JUST LIKE
YOU AND ME

JUST LIKE YOU AND ME

JOHNNY MORRIS

ILLUSTRATED BY

Sylvia Gainsford

BISHOPSGATE PRESS
37 Union Street,
London, SE1 1SE.

Jacket photograph of Johnny Morris
by permission of Marc Henri

© 1985 Johnny Morris

ISBN 0 900873 66 3

All enquiries and requests relevant to this title
should be sent to the publisher,
Bishopsgate Press Ltd., 37 Union Street, London SE1 1SE.

Printed by Whitstable Litho Ltd.,
Millstrood Road, Whitstable, Kent.

Contents

How to straighten out a python

It is, of course, an accepted fact that snakes are not everyone's cup of tea and are generally considered to be nasty pots of venom. I must confess that I am not all that mad about them; however you cannot help but admire their wonderful colouring and fascinating method of locomotion. I had always thought that snakes were impossible to understand but once you get to know them, you soon become familiar with their strange little ways.

Well, there was a pair of royal pythons at Bristol Zoo who had not eaten for 22 months, and getting to know animals that have not eaten for that length of time takes some doing – at least 22 months. What was the matter with them? Were they ill? Were they malingering, or just in the depths of a deep snake sulk? No, they were simply not eating: a fairly common occurrence among sliders, twisters and winders. But of course, they had to eat sooner or later, and they decided to eat later. But 22 months was rather a long time in-between courses.

These royal pythons were more or less the first snakes that I had ever handled. They were not large snakes, not more than six feet long, but I found them very gentle and quite friendly. They wound around my waist giving the suggestion that I was putting on a bit of weight here and there. Then they gently tested the circumference of my neck to make sure that I still took size 16 in collars. They peered into my face and stuck out their tongues at me while all the time I felt this uncanny but gentle pressure as they twined around me playing their crafty game of snakes and ladders. Royal pythons are well known for their docile nature, and I have even heard them described as cowardly snakes. When they are threatened they roll themselves up into a ball, consequently they are sometimes known as ball pythons.

I once met a taxi-driver who had a royal python. (Oh yes, you will find snake lovers and keepers in all walks of life). But

the pride and joy of his life was a boa constrictor and he was
heart broken then he had to get rid of it.

'Why did you get rid of it,' I asked.

'Well it was the missus see.'

'Oh, she didn't like it?'

'Oh yes,' he replied, 'she liked it but it kept getting in to the
sofa, see.'

It is true that snakes do seem to like getting into sofas and
it can be a bit unnerving to feel the sofa, on which you are
sitting, gently surge beneath you.

'The missus said the snake must go,' the taxi-driver
continued. 'Still I found it a good home you know, 'cos I
wouldn't sell it to a stripper or anything like that'.

'Not to a stripper. Why?'

'Well strippers keep their snakes in the fridge'.

Ah! It was obvious. Snakes become very active in the
warm and could get a little excited in the warm, smoky, drum-
thumping atmosphere of a strip club, and so they are cooled-
off in the fridge. This cooling-off makes them sluggish, lazy
and very dopey as you never want to do a strip act with a warm
python. On the other hand, it is a most cruel thing to keep a
snake in a fridge and so my taxi-driver had the right idea –
never sell your boa constrictor (or python) to a stripper!

Snakes do become more active in the warm and that is
why they become a little lively in television studios under the
hot lights. It is important therefore, to find out the character of
the snake you are going to handle.

One day a twelve foot python was brought to the studio by
a snake handler and his mate whom I had known for many
years; he was very quick to give me a brief rundown on the
nature of the beast.

'What's he like?' I naturally asked.

'Well, er, I don't know,' the handler replied.

'You don't know?'

'No, well its not my python. Mine's turned a bit funny and
I borrowed this one from a friend. Well, I didn't want to let
anybody down,' explained the consciencious handler.

'Mmmm . . . I don't like the look of this one.' I spoke warily as there were indications that he was not a very happy snake.

'Well, he's been alright with me so far',

'Mmm, so far. Alright, let's rehearse'.

The lights were very warm and taking the snake, I soon realised that he was far from happy as he was making a threatening noise, *haaa haaa*. It was being perfectly friendly warning kind friends one and all, 'leave me alone *haa haa*.,

Now the object of the programme was to demonstrate the movement of legless creatures; I was asked to hold the snake on a large trestle table and, if possible, straighten him out to his full length. There is one thing that snakes do not like above everything else in this world, and that is to be held out straight: to try to straighten out a warm, unhappy python was quite simply asking for it, and I got it. He bit me in the arm. I must say this in his favour, he didn't hang on to my arm but let go at once. However, his teeth had penetrated a thick jacket, a pullover and a shirt.

It was a most peculiar experience, for I knew that he was going to bite and there was nothing that I could do about it. His lunge was not particularly quick, almost done in slow motion, and yet I couldn't get my arm out of the way but unusually, I didn't feel a thing. My arm was beautifully punctured in two places. Well, the snake had warned us all but we ignored his warning. So he bit me but it was only a warning bite. He had done his best to tell us that to persevere with such an unhappy but reasonable animal would be nothing short of madness.

Now television studios are strange places in many ways and if you are a performer your only means of communication is through a floor manager who is usually an active, lively person who has, at times, to hop about quite a bit. He wears headphones and has a radio-mike. On this occasion, he was standing quite close to me and speaking into his microphone.

'No, no, well we got a bit of bother here, can't go on for a minute . . . yeah, yeah, well hang on'. Clearly the director in the gallery had not seen the difficulties we were in. 'Yeah, yeah, well I'll ask him. Yeah, yeah, would you try to do that again Johnny'.

'Not on your life', I replied. This is a very unhappy snake and I've got a wife and family to support'.

The snake handler and his mate were most upset by the behaviour of the python. 'I wouldn't have believed it, he has been as good as gold with me'. 'Yes', I countered, 'but he was cold then and is nicely warmed up now'.

'But what are we going to do'.

'We'll just have to drop the item, I replied'.

'Oh dear, oh dear, I feel I've let everybody down', moaned the handler. 'I tell you what I could do. I could sellotape his mouth up'.

'No, certainly not. I'll have nothing to do with it'.

Meanwhile the floor manager was still in consultation with the gallery. 'Yeah, yeah, yeah, well we've got this bit of bother . . . yeah, yeah'.

I remember reflecting on my stupidity in ignoring the snake's warnings when I looked towards the handler and his mate. They were out of vision behind the cameras. The handler had the python on his shoulders and I saw to my horror that his mate was about to put some sellotape around the python's mouth. All I was able to say was, 'Don't! don't!' for the python suddenly whipped his body around the handler's neck and constricted.

I suppose the handler remained vertical for about 7 seconds and by the time we got to him, he was flat on his back and unconscious. I had no idea that a constrictor is such an efficient piece of machinery. Every centimetre of the handler's neck was covered by the hard constricting muscle. The oxygen and blood supply to the brain had simply been cut off. We managed to prize the tail straight and the python's lock was broken. The handler recovered almost as quickly as he had succumbed. But the snake was still making his warning noise, 'haaa haaa . . . well I told you so I warned you'.

The floor manager was talking to the gallery who still

11

hadn't seen the drama of this throttling. 'Yeah, yeah, well —
no, we still got this bit of bother here. Yeah, but we'll
straighten it out'.

As I say, it's not wise to try to straighten out a warm
python but sometimes when it's a matter of life and death, its
jolly well very necessary.

The voice of India

"The voice of India so 'tis said is the voice of the Tiger". I have never heard it in the wild but have often heard it in zoos. It can be a most plaintive sound rather like someone with the gripes: *oooh oooh oooh,* you do sometimes get *waaaa,* but more often than not it is the former.

The other voice of India that I got to know very well was the voice of the Indian Hill Mynah. I got him many years ago when he was a few months old. He was a most handsome bird with the distinct blue—black, shiny plumage and the yellow wattle around his neck: we called him Dicklow. Why Dicklow you may wonder. Well I had an idea that it was a Romany word for neckerchief or scarf and Dicklow had a certain gypsy style about him. A certain 'what the heck, I don't care: go and chase yourself attitude'.

Almost immediately, he began making very human noises. Nothing intelligible as there was not a word that you could recognise — it was the general noise of several people talking at the same time, *blahblahblahblah hahahaha,* and he seemed to revel in cocktail parties speaking in long bursts, blahblahblahhahaha. We tried hard to teach him words and a few short sentences but he would have nothing to do with us. As his perch was quite close to the telephone he soon started to say 'Hello'. And he had several different 'Hellos'. There was an enquiring 'hello' and a welcoming 'hello', and 'I'm glad to say hello . . . '. The only words that he learnt directly from me were the ones which I greeted him with every morning, simply, 'good morning'. If you dropped a spoon or let the potatoes boil over he would say, 'good morning'. He meant, 'there you go again and the best of luck good morning'. Then he began to imitate the laughter of my wife and I, *ha ha ha ha hahahaha.* His timing was perfect, *Ha ha ha ha hahahaha.*

Then in the dreadful winter of 1962 he suddenly said something quite awful, and I couldn't have taught these words

13

to him in a hundred years, I honestly do not think that I said them in front of him more than a few times. We had had a snow fall and it lay about two feet deep all around us, and every time I shovelled a pathway to the coalhouse the wind blew and filled it in again. Consequently, every morning I had to shovel it clear again. I do remember coming in, easing my wellies off and saying, 'I don't know, I'm blankity blank if I know'. But obviously that was all Dicklow needed as he was on it like a shot. His pronunciation and clarity of that profanity was remarkable. 'I'm blankity blank if I know'. Thank goodness he didn't use it very often but when he did it was devastating.

In the summer Dicklow lived in the garden. We had a cage and the bottom of it had been removed so that he could peck about in the grass and eventually we let him go free in the garden while we got on with the hoeing and the dead heading of the roses. Dicklow liked making little heaps of stones then, from time to time laughing at what he had done.

One afternoon a gentleman from the Conservative Party called for old things for the Summer Fayre. Dicklow was collecting stones and saying, 'good morning, hello'. The gentleman was most interested as he had never seen or heard a bird like ours before.

'What sort of bird is that' he enquired politely.

'A mynah bird' I replied.

'A what — a mynah bird'.

Oh! Where do they come from?'.

Dicklow knew the answer to that one, 'I'm blankety blanked if I know'.

'Good heavens. Did you hear what that bird said'.

'I'm very much afraid I did. Sorry' I apologised.

'Good heavens. Do they swear like that in the wild?' our visitor enquired.

Dicklow thought that was very funny, '*Ha ha ha ha hahahaha' that in the wild.*

Can you imagine a mynah bird getting up in the morning saying; 'Cor, I had a rotten night last night. Well the missus made the nest didn't she; blinking twigs sticking in me back.

I'm blankity blanked if I know'.

Dicklow would sometimes fly about but flying is not a Mynah's strong point. Every flight they make looks like their first flight and they look really frightened when they are flying as though they are out of petrol and are going to crash land. But one day Dicklow really took off. Unfortunately there was a pretty strong breeze blowing and it carried him beyond the trees, and he was gone. We rushed out into the lane to see where he was going but were too late. He'd disappeared and there was not a sign of him. Next to the lane was a field of wheat which was waist high and there was about fifty acres of it. We walked carefully and slowly through the wheatfield. We had given up hope of ever seeing him again when we heard him laughing, *ha ha ha ha hah.* It was funny to hear laughter from a field of wheat. One imagines a courting couple lying there hidden and then getting a bit skittish. We soon located Dicklow and he hopped onto my shoulder and we returned to the garden with Dicklow laughing all the way back. *Ha ha ha ha hahahah.*

Shortly after this I made my first journey to India to accompany a white tiger. White tigers are very rare and are extremely beautiful animals. They are the colour of Siamese cats and yes, they have got blue eyes too. In the past when they were sighted in the wild, they were usually shot as they were considered to be a bad omen or the ghost of an evil spirit. It did not matter what the circumstances were, they were done away with until a certain Maharajah collected a pair and bred from them; British zoos acquired a few of the progeny and in turn bred from them as did the Delhi Zoo in India. But the zoo in Delhi produced lots of males while the zoo in Bristol produced lots of females. Obviously there had to be an exchange, and so a female was to be sent from Bristol and a male brought back from Delhi. We set off with the tiger, a veterinary surgeon and a camera crew.

She was a most beautiful tiger, about two years old and not a bit concerned with what was going on. Born and bred in a zoo, she had every confidence in those humans who were

around her. We had, of course, to take her to the freight department at the airport and when we got there, there was just a little reluctance to let us know what was going on.

'We are very sorry to say that the plane will be late'.

'Oh dear, we've got a tiger here you know'.

'Yes, yes, I know but everything I'm sure will be alright'.

'But how late will the plane be?'

'I shouldn't think very long'. And so this discourse went on, little knowing that the plane was sitting at Kennedy Airport in New York having a new engine fitted. We waited and the tiger waited. She talked to us with that funny horse noise that tiger's make *phhllll*; and gradually the whole place became deserted.

I have noticed in the past, when things go wrong with an airliner, everyone disappears, and you have great difficulty in contacting the staff. The freight department had slyly emptied itself of all forms of human life save for our camera crew, the vet, the producer and myself. Then I spotted someone just sneaking through the door into the freight department. It was the gentleman we had initially spoken to.

'I say'.

'Oh! Mr. Morris you are still here'.

'Looks like it doesn't it', I replied.

'Oh! Yes, have you heard the news?'

'No, what news?' 'The plane has been so badly delayed and you will not be able to fly until tomorrow'.

'Not until tomorrow?'

'No I'm very sorry but we have arranged hotel accommodation for all of you'.

'But if we are not to leave until tomorrow, we will have lost a whole day's filming; do you realise we will have lost a whole day'.

'Oh! Don't worry Mr. Morris, perhaps the same thing will happen at the other end and you will get that whole day back again'.

'Oh! hahah. Yes. Very true, very true'.

Just then the tiger roared, *Ooohoooh*.

'Ah, Mr. Morris the voice of India'. The voice of India! I would say that India has lots of voices, there's *RAAAA* and *OOOH OOOH* and *Ha ha ha hahahaha*.

The amateur photographer

Those of you who are interested in photography might do well to spend an hour or two watching an orang-utan at work taking photographs. He is quite the most cunning operator I know. He does not have a camera, of course, but nonetheless he photographs you. Approach an orang-utan and he will look the other way but he senses you are there. He will probably haul himself up on his legs and start to climb the bars of his cage and at some point during his climb, he will cast you a glance in just one twenty-fifth of a second. It is a most casual glance done in a most off-hand way, then he looks the other way as though you were just not worth worrying about. He has photographed you and knows exactly what he is going to do when you get close enough as he has worked out his plan of campaign. First, he photographs you and therefore knows whether you are wearing glasses as he is going to have those off in a couple of ticks. If you are wearing a tie he will try and choke you with it. If you are wearing a decent sort of suit he will regurgitate his food over you just for fun. I know, as I have had all these things done to me many, many times.

Orangs know exactly how to embarrass you. They are masters at it. There was a very fine looking orang called Oscar. Oscar was about five years old and he came to the studio every week from Bristol zoo. He was not put into a cage but was placed on a climbing frame in the middle of the studio and everything was removed from his reach. He was isolated on a climbing-frame island as orangs, especially young ones, do not like wide open spaces but prefer to have things on which to cling. And so, Oscar was very happy to twirl around on his climbing frame waiting for the programme to start but all the time he would be photographing everything and everyone that moved in the studio. A boom microphone swung overhead. He photographed it and looked the other way as though he could not care less, not wanting to have anything to do with booms.

Suddenly that long ginger arm would shoot out and bang, he had got it. Then the tussle would start. It is not easy to get a microphone away from an orang-utan especially if he wants to eat it.

In the days of Oscar, our programme was transmitted live and every week. Before the programme started, I used to have a word or two with Oscar just to let him explore the suit I was wearing and to let him have a good sniff around to see if I had picked up any interesting smells during the past week. He always photographed me, of course, the moment I came through the studio door: one twenty-fifth of a second and then he would look the other way to work out his little plan.

Now on one particular day, I had cut my little finger, not badly, but I had put a small piece of flesh-coloured tape over it. Oscar photographed me and then looked the other way; I went over to him. He pretended to be looking up at the boom but his long ginger arm stretched out and took my hand. He lifted it to his nose and smelt the band of tape around my little finger. 'Hello hello, what have you been doing to yourself. Cut yourself ain't you. Smells a bit of antiseptic that tape. Think we just better have it off don't you'. Very carefully, and with tremendous interest, he slowly peeled the tape off my finger. Such are the powers of observation of the orang-utan and their incredible ability to work things out and improvise. Oscar had spotted that bit of tape when I was several yards away, he knew it would come off and he took it off.

The scale of an operation does not deter an orang. I know of a certain zoo where they re-turfed the orangs' outside enclosure. Then they let them out onto the lovely green turfed enclosure, but a bit too soon, before the turfs had really bonded to the ground. Those orangs rolled up all the turf far faster than it was put down in the first place and then stacked the turf in the corner where it had previously been stacked. The orang-utans had watched the men put the turf down and had photographed the whole operation in detail. They knew exactly what to do. Never to underestimate the ability of inventiveness of an orang-utan.

Oscar too, was full of surprises and on one occasion I wondered how he would react toward a lady zoologist who was coming to the studio. Now natural science on the television screen should be a proper blend of science and entertainment but it is not always so by a long chalk. A recital of scientific facts can be as entertaining as a railway timetable. But it was thought that Oscar was far too entertaining and it was about time someone spilled the scientific facts about him. And so here enters the lady zoologist. But before going live on camera we thought that we had better just have a quick rehearsal with Oscar and her together. I couldn't believe it. He didn't put a foot wrong. He lay in her arms as good as gold as she said, 'Well now, here we have an orang-utan, it is also known as the old man of the woods. It is an arboreal animal that means it lives in the trees. Now the females and the young usually live in groups while the adult males live solitary lives. They come from Sumatra and from Borneo'.

Oscar was fascinated, he had never heard so much about himself ever before. He lay there, looking up at her face, as good as gold. True, he did at one point probe her left nostril with his index finger but for an orang that's nothing. We put him back on to his climbing frame and as our rehearsal had gone so well, we decided to have a cup of tea and come back for the programme.

I was waiting in the studio when the lady zoologist came in through the doors. I saw Oscar photograph her and then he twirled around his climbing frame in a very carefree way. He had seen what I had seen. Well at rehearsal the lady zoologist was wearing a pullover and jeans but for the live transmission she had changed her clothes completely and was now wearing a very nice blouse with a most attractive full skirt. Sudden changes of clothes can get you into a lot of trouble with orang-utans but Oscar was a young orang and was fairly gentle. I thought that he should be alright but orangs are full of surprises.

I talked to him on his climbing frame, you know all the old rubbish. 'Now you're going to be good aren't you, Oscar.

23

You're not going to play up are you? Ah, that's alright mate I knew I could trust old Oscar couldn't I'.

But I could see that he was photographing that skirt over and over again. There was still a little bit of film left to run before Oscar's piece: time enough for me to get Oscar off his climbing frame and hand him over to the lady zoologist. He was very, very good, lying there in her arms just as he had done at rehearsal. And their item began.

'Well now here we have an orang-utan it is also known as the old man of the woods. It is an arboreal animal that means it lives in the trees'.

It was then that Oscar started to move. He was going down on to the floor, there was no doubt at all about that. She tried to stop him but orangs are made of mahogany and elastic and when they want to do something, they are certainly going to do it. I could see what he was going to do and he did it. He lifted the lady's very full skirt and, like an old fashioned photographer, went underneath it. She tried to get him out. Nothing doing.

I was standing out of shot beside the camera. If I attempted to get Oscar out it could produce a much more embarrassing situation than the one we were already in. There was nothing that anyone could do. It was like watching someone frantically drowning. She struggled on.

'Now the females and the young usually live in groups while the adult males live solitary lives. They come from Sumatra and Borneo'.

It was hilarious. For once science was being more entertaining than an entertainer could ever be and all thanks to Oscar's fine photographic ability. He had photographed that skirt the moment he saw it. In a world of jumpers and jeans, he had never seen a skirt before but he knew exactly what to do about it. As you photographers say, and as Oscar will agree, 'Yes it always pays to have your camera with you'.

Lion enters left: exits right

It is sometimes extremely difficult indeed to impress upon people that you cannot make animals do things that they don't want to to. Well, of course, in some cases you can but that is only by careful training. To simply write a film-shooting script and in a lordly way expect and insist that an animal must comply is just plain barmy. I once saw, many years ago, a film script and the director had written, 'lion enters left: exits right'. Well you have got to have a fair bit of luck to achieve that for even if the lion does walk from left to right you may be sure that when it does, the camera man will not be ready. Then even if the lion does walk from left to right and the camera man is ready, chances are that there will be a Boeing 747 a few hundred feet overhead making sound recording impossible.

Now I don't want to keep on, but suppose that everything works fairly well, you can still get a hair in the gate. This is a nasty affliction that happens to cameras or you can get something much worse, a bird's nest. A hair in the gate is simply a hair that gets itself trapped between the lens of the camera and the film; a bird's nest is something that happens when the film becomes really unruly and does not wind itself properly from one spool to another. It goes, *bbyyyahsluckclunk,* simply jams solid and you have got a bird's nest. There are many other things that can go wrong. The light can go up or down, one of those gawping stupid faces can suddenly appear just out of focus and grin like a mad thing straight into the camera, or you can get boom shadow. Boom shadow is simply the shadow cast by the boom microphone and has a quality all of its own. Should you by the rarest chance get your lion to enter left and exit right, by the time its halfway through its walk, a boom shadow will have quietly slipped into place. The boom shadow is a proper will-o-the-wisp. It haunts every film studio, taunts and mocks those that ask lions to walk from left to right.

At the end of a frustrating day after imposing your rotten little will on a lion by asking it to enter left and exit right, you will have on your hands a lion who is distinctly cheesed off and could be approaching a state where he is going to give somebody a four penny one. Trained animals, of course, can be asked to do things in spite of bird's nests and boom shadows but even the most amenable of them will revolt at times.

Trained animals when they have had enough will say enoughs. I once met two killer whales. Both of them were incredible animals weighing about 3 tons each. They both performed that most spectacular leap for a ball hung high over their pool. To effect this jump, they had first to dive to the bottom of their deep pool and then drive upwards, their great tails pumping away until they had enough momentum to surge their three tons out of the water, and just tip the ball hung twenty-five feet above the pool. It is a breathtaking sight.

On this particular occasion, they had already given several performances when we asked the trainer if they would do it again for the camera. They did it again. The cameraman said that he wasn't sure whether he had got it right, could they possibly do it again. So they did it again, and again, and just to be sure, they did it again. They had had enough but the male was willing to try once more. I watched him go into his dive, he got to the bottom, turned to drive up when the female crossed his path and stopped him. 'No dear, not again, we've done enough for one day'.

This last illustration lets you see why I was very wary when approached by an advertising company's executive and asked to appear in a television advertisement with two cows: one a Jersey and the other a Guernsey.

'This is in the open-air, in a field?' I naturally asked.

'No, its in a film studio'.

'Oh dear!'

'Why oh dear?'

'Well I don't suppose that these cows have ever been in a film studio'.

'Does that make any difference?'

'They could go bananas and no doubt you've only got the studio for a day'. I said wistfully.

'Well, yes, we will easily do it in a day', the executive concluded.

Now the advertisement was for milk – good quality milk. The idea was to make the studio look like a sea of milk and yours truly, was to walk onto this sea of milk leading the Jersey and the Guernsey: do a small spiel and that would be that. I explained to the executive and his crew that they would need cows that were used to wearing halters and being led. The cows also had to know and be used to one another, for cows, like human beings, can be spiteful and vicious. Full credit to the ad boys for they found two cows on a large farm, one Jersey and one Guernsey, and they asked the stockman to walk them every day, the Guernsey on the left and the Jersey on the right. The stockman said that they also shared the same stall and were getting on wonderfully. He trained them methodically, and when he brought them along to the film studio I could see that they were beautifully turned out and, thank goodness, as quiet as well-trained show cattle have to be.

The studio wasn't quite ready for us as they were still spraying the walls and floor a lovely, creamy white. The cows waited patiently until we were ready to go.

'Lots of banging and crashing. Chaps stop shouting out. Can we have it quiet there, quiet please'. The cows didn't seem to mind. 'Alright action', the producer shouted.

I walked on to the studio floor with the cows following me like lambs. This was really going to be a piece of cake. Unfortunately, the cows had never walked on a hollow wooden white-painted floor before, and it frightened them. They didn't jump about or anything like that, they just did what cows always do when they are a bit unnerved. We all know that familiar cow-shed noise. My Uncle Percy used to do a perfect imitation of it at Christmas parties. He would stand on the linoleum floor and with a pack of playing cards in each hand, he would say *Moo* then dribble the cards slowly from his hands on to the floor. Aunties and Uncles used to fall about

28

laughing. Percy was really awful. Well, we got Uncle Percy's special effect that morning. The gentleman in charge of studio decorating was appalled, 'Oh no! We'll have to spray the whole lot again'.

The studio was in a mess and we had to wait for it to be resprayed. This time the director said, 'look I want to change the cows over – the Jersey looks better on the other side'.

'You can't do that'.

'I want to try' insisted the director.

WELL, we tried it and the cows didn't like it. We got a long encore of Uncle Percy's party trick. 'Oh no, we'll have to spray the whole lot again', said the studio decorator.

Now a respray is much worse than a hair in the gate or a bird's nest – a respray takes a long time as the paint has got to dry. But such was the lovely nature of these porcelain-like cows that they didn't complain. After several resprays, we got the shots we wanted.

However, some directors know no bounds. 'Right, now I want the cows to lie down side by side; make them lie down will you'.

'But I can't make them lie down'.

'Look it's here in the script', insisted the director.

'But I can't make them lie down', the stockman said, 'they will lie down sometime today, sir. You can't make 'em lay down. If you tried you'd be here respraying all night. There's only one way that might work. Put some straw under them turn out all the lights and go away'.

'Oh, very well, I'll give them an hour'.

Within 40 minutes these two darlings had laid themselves down, side-by-side, looking like a dream on that sea of white milk. Some time later I saw the advertisement and it really did look beautiful. We were very lucky for we didn't get a hair in the gate, or a bird's nest but I thought I detected on that milk white sea just the faintest smudge of a boom shadow. Or was it?

Suck it and see

The fountain of knowledge and all the facts and figures that pour from it are eagerly sought by many people. There are those who are gluttons for knowledge. The trouble with knowledge is that it is red hot. Those that gather it cannot hold it for any length of time. They can't keep it to themselves, they have got to get rid of it. Their knowledge pours out with the same generosity as the fountain by which they were drenched. Well perhaps it's not all generosity. They have to spout it all out, from time to time, to make sure that they have remembered their knowledge correctly. And, like the Ancient Mariner, *"who stoppeth one of three"*, they will do just that to make sure that you know exactly the tremendous advantages of a prehensile tail to a spider monkey, or the fine attributes of the enormous ears of the fennec fox. They never speculate on the fun that it would be if we had prehensile tails, and could swing about on the chandeliers in the Covent Garden opera house during the Twilight of the Gods, which is what I have always wanted to do in such a situation. For Wagner deliberately wrote music to drive some of us up the twist, or into the chandeliers to behave like spider monkeys with prehensile tails.

Let us ponder for a moment or two on what a great luxury it would be if we had ears like the fennec fox. Imagine travelling on British Rail in the middle of the summer when the thermostat goes wrong, yet again, and the heat comes full on. Those beautiful large ears would keep us wonderfully cool and we could flick them about all the way from Paddington to Exeter. But our ears have no dual purpose; they are there to hear. One bit of our ear does seem completely useless: the lobe. The lobe of the ear doesn't seem to do a lot to earn it's keep. It seems that if we want to do something useful with our ear lobes we just bung a hole in them and hang a bit of gold through it with perhaps a diamond dangling on the end. Although sometimes, just sometimes, the old lobe of the ear is quite useful when you have a problem to solve. Nothing too difficult such as 'Now let's see where shall I put those daffodil bulbs along the hedge there, or around the tree'. You will find that a tug or two on the left-hand lobe is like ringing for the butler and will produce a positive response.

I suppose I subconsciously associated the ears of the fennec fox with with railway trains because it was in a railway train that as a very small boy I first learned to flap my ears. The train was travelling at quite a smart lick when it dived into a tunnel. The variation of pressure on my little old lugs sent them flat against my head, they flapped. Then a sudden bang as we went through the tunnel; somehow this released the prehistoric muscles around my ears and set them working. Thereafter, I was easily the best ear flapper in the school. I practised hard, the ear muscles grew strong and woe betide any fly that landed on my right ear, which was my strongest, he was flicked away and sent crashing into the wall; such is the value of ears and tails.

Tails are thought by many to be very pretty attachments. They keep off the flys, help you keep on an even keel while acting as a balancing pole, and some tails look as though they could ring a peal of bells. I refer, of course, to the beautiful peppermint-striped tails of the ring-tail lemur. A ring tailed lemur's tail looks just like the 'sally' on a bell rope. To see a group of sixty to seventy of these dear little animals sitting in a tree looks for all the world like a miniature belfry. I once saw in the south of France. There lived a gentleman who had a bit of a fixation on lemurs of all sorts, but his favourites were the ring-tailed lemurs and he had well over sixty of them, and they were all but a few months old. They were, of course, for sale and we had gone there to choose a young female for the Bristol Zoo and take her back with us. The lemurs were all in spanking condition and as lively as twanging elastic. And you could not tell one from the other. I will never forget going into one enclosure with about twenty lemurs. You soon become smothered in lemurs as they are very fond of human

perspiration. They love undoing shoe laces, and are good at picking pockets. They came bounding out of the trees one after the other; it was a glorious playtime. But the playtime had to come to an end, and we chose a little lemur and christened her Dotty. A ghastly pun I'm afraid on the name of a famous film star, Dorothy Lamour. Dorothy Lemur became Dotty.

We had a very smart and convenient little crate for her and set off for home but calling first at Paris. Now we had to stay in Paris for a day or two as we wanted to do some work at the Paris Zoo. The Paris hotel was small but pleasant: and my room had a small bathroom. It was midsummer and very, very warm and so I left the windows open. Dotty was in her crate in the bathroom and I made her a nice assorted dish of fruit salad. I opened the door of her crate and wondered. Her brown eyes almost glowed from the gloom of her crate. She was wondering too. Where was she, what were we doing to her? Where were all the other lemurs? Where were the palm trees and the sunshine? What is this, a dish of fruit? A dish of fruit well that's something. She put out her hand and took a slice of apple. A lemur's hand is one of the little miracles of the animal world for it is just like your hand or mine, wonderfully proportioned but tiny. She sat on her haunches eating her apple and then a grape but she did not want to come out of her crate. What was out there was very strange to her and it smelt of soap, so she decided to stay in her crate. She had all but finished her fruit, had a drink of water, and stared at me until I closed the little crate door. I read for a while and went to bed and to sleep.

It was about one in the morning when I realised there was a bit of a rumpus going on in the bathroom. Dotty was banging about in her crate clearly in distress, and going, *waaa waaa*. Well now, what do we do? Lemurs are partly nocturnal and would rather like to be up and about doing something. I knew that I would have to do something and so I closed the windows and put all breakable stuff, such as ash trays and clocks, in the wardrobe. I opened the door of the crate and left it open so that Dotty could come out if she wanted to. After about 10 minutes she did. I lay in bed and I watched her come out of the bathroom very, very carefully, looking around with a wonderful moon-struck stare. 'Hello Dotty you alright'. She saw me lying in bed and with a tremendous leap she was on the pillow. I shall never forget the wonderful way she adapted herself to her strange surroundings. She slipped into bed and wriggled close to my face, and with her two tiny hands she took the lobe of my ear and sucked it. She had spotted in a minute the use of the lobe of the human ear to lemurs. As far as I know she sucked it all night because when I woke in the morning she was half asleep but the lobe of my ear was still in her little mouth. It had been her comforter. After all she had been dragged away from her brothers and sisters and was totally alone and at a loss. Her solace and comfort lay in the lobe of a human ear. Dottie and I have been close friends now for over 20 years. So when the fountain of knowledge starts spouting on about the versatility of the ears of the fennec fox, I am always able to say that there is a good deal more to the human ear than meets the eye. Especially to a ring-tail lemur.

A nice quiet meal

There are those who are convinced that perhaps the greatest luxury in the world is to dine by candlelight. A couple of spluttering candles are supposed to convince you that a burning romance is at any moment, about to set you on fire. You can hardly blame us for we are bombarded with pamphlets from travel companies telling us that we really haven't lived unless we go to so and so and enjoy the luxury of a nice quiet meal by candlelight. Well it is a bit unfortunate for me because a dripping candle reminds me of my childhood and of the outside lavatory that stood so alone on the other side of the backyard. To be simply forced to stumble out there on a cold winter's night and light the candle, trembling as the black shadows played with the wobbling ghosts on the wall. No, a quiet dinner by candlelight is just not for me, I much prefer a noisy lunch in broad daylight: and so do gorillas. Gorillas simply love a good noisy meal — talk about snap, crackle, pop!

There was, and still is, a beautifully mannered gorilla at Bristol Zoo. The first time I met her, she hit me. I knew she was going to hit me because when a gorilla is about to do you mischief it turns its lips inwards in a very menacing sneer, which so definitely says 'Cor you ain't half going to cop it'. And you do. Wallop. It wasn't a knock out punch, and as so often happens, then she galloped to the other side of the cage and sat down to consider what sort of tactics she would employ for round two. I didn't give her very long to consider as I could be in for a bit of a rough and tumble. There was a sort of scrubbing brush in the cage and I picked it up, went over to her, and bopped her one with it. She was most surprised and a little hurt, not physically but psychologically. I went back to my corner, the blue corner and left her sitting in the red corner; end of round one. Round two coming up.

For the first thirty seconds of round two neither of us moved. She glared at me considering what to do next; and I

knew that she would do something soon. Fortunately, I remembered that I had a couple of apples in my pockets. Very hard, sweet Cox's Orange Pippins. I took a very noisy bite at one of them, *crrrrk,* and ignored her but I could see out of the corner of my eye that she simply could not stand the noise of a Cox's Orange Pippin being crunched up. *Crrk crrk crrk.* It was agony for her.

She forced herself to get up and slowly came over to me. She eyed the scrubbing brush beside me carefully and then sat on it. She stared at me with that incredible, dignified longing look that gorillas can put on at times. But there was no attempt to snatch the apple I was eating, oh no, she was now perfectly behaved. I took out the other apple and gave it to her. She didn't snatch at it but took it like the vicar's wife taking a cream cake. However she did make much more noise than the vicar's wife, *champ chompchomp.* That gorilla's name was Delilah. She still lives at Bristol Zoo with the group of gorillas that the zoo has very skilfully formed during the past 15 years or so.

In the bad old days, the only way to supply a gorilla to a zoo was to go to Africa, shoot the mother gorilla and bring the baby back. It was not until 1956 that the first ever baby gorilla was born in captivity. Previously they were all caught in the wild and brought back to zoos. In the wild, these poor, little babies spend a lot of time clinging to their mother's chests. The contact between Mother and baby is warm and close, with a good old heart beat of comfort softly thudding away. When that contact is broken the infant is at a loss, and so whoever is looking after one of these poor little unfortunates will be received with a lot of affection and boisterous play. Of course, that is fine when the gorilla is small but when he grows and becomes larger, he does not want his keeper to leave him. A young gorilla will block his keeper's way, holding him tight: in fact, holding him captive for they are, even as youngsters, incredibly strong. But even in a great mountain of strength lies a great weakness. Gorillas are most easily frightened by strange tiny objects. Suddenly produce a small doll and the

great gorilla will run off and cower in a corner. In the old days, that was the only way a keeper could get out of a gorilla's cage. Of course you could not do that too often, because if the gorilla got used to the doll he would no longer be frightened by it. But some small things they never get used to.

Miss Molly Badham, who created that very fine zoo at Twycross, had a young gorilla. He was a wonderful looking animal and totally devoted to Molly. She fed him, played with him, and she had a special bed made for him in her bedroom. In the daytime she would bring him downstairs and drive him in her mini-van to his special enclosure in the zoo where he used to amuse himself throwing lumps of this and that at the dear general public. At the end of the day when Molly came with the mini-van, he would sit in the passenger seat like any city gent and be driven home. Now Molly is a very compact, petite person and to see her driving the van with this enormous black gorilla sitting beside her was really quite a sight. When they got to Molly's home they would both get out of the van and go through the front door into the rather large hallway. [I promise you that this is true for I saw it happen myself.] As they entered the hall a very smart pussy cat came from the kitchen and sat down calmly cleaning herself at the bottom of the stairs. This great gorilla, who was then nine years old, would not go near that cat. He literally rolled his eyes with a dreadful apprehension. He was scared stiff of that cat, and he never got used to her. Whenever Molly and he came home, that clever pussy cat would time things exactly so that at some point she would be found either dawdling at the foot of the stairs cleaning its left leg on the half landing, or in Molly's bedroom sitting on her bed. It was a calculated pussy cat ploy. 'Who did that great black gorilla think he was, he daren't come near me'. It worked for he never did. She always placed herself in front of the gorilla and every day that pussy cat had to be physically removed: such are the relative strengths of gorillas and pussy cats. Gorillas as they say just don't know their own strength while pussy cats, it seems do.

Delilah my Cox's Orange Pippin friend at the Bristol Zoo

grew to be a very fine lady, and I went to see her a few months after she had her first baby, taking a noisy picnic lunch with me. Thank heavens she was nursing her baby herself which was an amazing bit of luck as zoo animals very often do not know what to do with their helpless offspring. Mind you, to see a gorilla mother with her child makes you think that she doesn't know what to do with it for she treats it in a most off-hand manner. When the child is not clinging to its mother's breast, mother will carry it around rather like a handbag swinging it, easily like a lady out window shopping. Delilah seemed quite pleased to see me for when I went into her cage and sat down she immediately came and sat on my lap which was quite a bit of a weight, I must admit. It is a rather unique situation to have a gorilla sitting on your lap and cradling her first baby in her arms. We talked of old times, how she hit me and how I hit her and of how we had made it up with a couple of Cox's Orange Pippins. Her big, thoughtful eyes now gazed at me with some affection. I wasn't quite happy though about the baby. His little head was lolling right back over his mother's arm. And so I said, 'Look don't you think it would be a good idea to support the little nipper's head. She looked at me and her look said, 'If you think you are so blinking clever you nurse him'. And Delilah handed me her baby who I nursed while she got on with her noisy lunch. First of all there were raw carrots: *chompchompchomp,* raw leeks: *crunchcrunch,* some delicious Cox's Orange Pippins: *crrk crrk crrk,* and two great sticks of celery: *crrkcrrkcrrk.* A very noisy lunch. So now you see why I'm not at all keen on a quiet candlelit dinner. Give me a noisy daylight lunch anytime.

41

A matter of tolerance

I remember well a very bad tempered schoolmaster who used to yell at the little naughty school children who he tried to control, 'I will not tolerate this sort of behaviour, I will not tolerate it'. Good word tolerate.

Animals too, have a way of saying I will not tolerate this sort of behaviour any more. They usually bite you, kick you or spit upon you. To be spat upon by a camel or a llama is a very telling experience, for the animal does not attempt to disguise its contempt for you. A kick is delivered, I always feel more out of irritation, and a bite is often just a warning. Of course, there are those who bite and kick such as the pretty striped Zebras and that means that they are going to kill you. They will not tolerate human beings.

I once met a most tolerant tiger. He was to appear with me in an advertisement and it was to be filmed in the open. It was also to be filmed in colour and on 35 mm film. Now a 35 mm camera is a pretty hefty affair and needs at least three people to work it. The cameraman, the operator, and the focus puller. With such a big camera the focussing is critical and the focus puller carries with him a tape measure. This he hooks on to the camera and measures the distance between the camera and the subject to be filmed. You will hear him murmur to himself, 'yeah 14 ft, 14 ft. He'll then adjust the camera and pull focus as and when required. It is not a wildly exciting job, and let me say here and now, just in case there may be some of you attracted to the glamour of film making, it is just about the most boring business I know. It is like being in the army, 95 per cent boring and 5 per cent exciting. You are always waiting, waiting, waiting. And then suddenly we are ready and people start to shout.

'Quiet, quiet everyone. Right let's have the tiger for rehearsal'.

'Look, please don't rehearse the tiger'.

'Why not?'

'Well he's got a tolerance of, at the most, I should say two minutes'.

'What's that mean?'

'Well if I've got to hold this tiger he'll go bananas in about two minutes and rip me to bits'.

'Oh! alright'.

So we rehearsed without the tiger. Now the plan was to start with a closeup right on the tiger's face then widen out to include yours truly as well. We rehearsed again and again and then brought on the tiger. He was a beauty. A big, very serious tiger cub of a few months old. I was to hold him in my arms where he settled most peacefully, looking around first at the camera crew, the camera and then up at the boom. It is fine when they are interested because they are quiet.

'Look we'd better get on'.

'Just a minute Harry, I don't like that shadow there. Can you take it out'.

Unfortunately, Harry came with a large reflector, angled it to the sun and the sun's reflection shone strong upon the tiger's face. He blinked a bit, I thought he would panic but he didn't, he was good, very, good. I kept talking to him and he seemed to be listening. But I knew that time must be running out.

'Quiet everyone, quiet everyone'.

Oh dear, please don't shout.

'Right stand by'.

The tiger was still very, very good. I kept talking to him. And then advancing towards us, in a trance, was the focus puller dragging his tape measure. The tiger watched him approach with great interest but he was still very, very good. The focus puller put the tape measure right on the tiger's nose and murmured, '16 feet', suddenly the tiger went *RAAA* and bit him on the hand that held the tape. The focus puller suddenly woke up.

Hey he bit me'.

'Afraid so — he won't tolerate that'. And that was the end

of shooting for a couple of hours while everybody calmed down and the tiger regained his tolerance.

I suppose the record for tolerance must go to Dotty, the ring-tailed lemur. Every week, for years and years, she was brought to the television studio at Bristol. I went into her little enclosure which was decorated with trees, and she always jumped from the tree onto my left shoulder. Brilliant — well not really. I always kept sweets and grapes in my left-hand jacket pocket and she was virtually trained to do it, let's say conditioned. Well much television was transmitted live in those days and to be able to predict what an animal was going to do was most useful for the director and the cameras. They knew just where to position themselves for dear little Dotty was totally predictable. She was hooked on chocolate drops and grapes but only on studio days, and on those days, without fail, she jumped lightly on to my left shoulder. There I fed her chocolate drops and grapes and she licked the sweat of my brow. Sometimes, if we were under-running, I would give her a whole banana as this took her quite a time to eat.

Despite the fact that she was a very tolerant creature. She just would not tolerate; being picked up. Try picking up Dotty and you would find yourself in the infirmary in no time at all as lemurs can most quickly and wonderfully bite. Even I, the cornucopia of chocolate drops and grapes, would not dream of picking her up. Dotty herself was once attacked by another lemur and she suffered a dreadful scar in the groin that must have been four inches long. The lemur bite is more of a rip; as first they dig their teeth in and then push with their strong back legs and leave you, as they jump away, with quite a gash.

Dotty had a many many children, often twins, and they too would come to the studio with her riding on her back, the spitting image of their mum. It was indeed a pretty sight; you could almost see those little lemurs grow week-by-week as their rate of growth is quite rapid and there soon comes a time when you simply could not tell the difference between mother and twins. The only way to tell was to see which one jumped onto the left shoulder and that would be Dotty for she knew where dwelt the chocolate drops and grapes. The twins would sit on my right shoulder and would get a choc drop and a grape every now and again but Dotty got the lion's share. I knew that if I could keep her on my left shoulder tucking away at the food that she would not jump back into the tree. And as long as Dotty stayed there the twins would stay too. It is easy to see now why things turned out the way they did. Well, the twins, physically were exactly the same as their mother but they were also developing their reasoning powers. And children of all sorts, seek eventually to test and then usurp parental authority. Unknown to me this state of affairs had arisen twixt Dotty and the twins. There was no outward sign that I could detect, although they were nattering to one another quite a bit. The plain fact was that the stronger of the twins, the male, was getting just a bit too macho and was telling his mother that she had had the good life for long enough sitting on my left shoulder and getting the lion's share of the choc drops and grapes and today, he was taking up his position on my left shoulder. So, when I went into their cage to close the programme I did not know that I had suddenly got the macho boy on my left shoulder and his sister and Dotty on my right. I fed the choc drops and grapes to the left shoulder and now and again, one to the right shoulder. Then I felt a little hand tapping my face from the right shoulder, but did not realise what it meant. It was Dotty, trying to tell me that she wasn't getting the amount of goodies to which she was normally entitled; suddenly, there was a short squeal and she bit me on the face.

I closed the programme that evening with 'Thats all for today, see you next week', blood streaming down my face. Dotty's tolerance had snapped. Like the old school master she had simply said, 'I will not tolerate this sort of behaviour, I will not tolerate it'. Like the tiger with the focus puller her tolerance had just snapped.

47

Three cheeky monkeys

We have a very dear friend called Charlie. A human animal who travels all over the world. He is a compulsive present giver and whenever he goes on one of his trips he comes back loaded with presents. Many years ago he came back, from goodness only knows where, with a great grin almost cutting his face in half.

'Hallo old boy'.

'Hallo Charlie. How's everything?'

'Fine, fine I've brought you a present'. Its for you and Eileen.'

'Charlie, you've brought us so many presents we'll have to build a garage or something'.

'Ah! but I've never ever brought a present like this one', he replied.

'What is it Charlie?'

'Wait till you see it — its a monkey'.

'I don't believe you Charlie'.

'I have, its a lovely monkey. I've got it in the car.

'Now look Charlie, we can't keep a monkey — nobody should keep monkeys; they break up the happy home in two ticks'.

'Ah! you'll like this one I'll go and get it'.

Moments later he came in carrying a box and at once I realised that as there were no ventilation holes in the box there couldn't be a live monkey in it. If it ever had been live then by now it was surely dead. It was a toy monkey, a big mechanical toy monkey, operated by a couple of batteries and playing a set of cymbals. When you pressed the switch it clonked these two cymbals together, *gang, gang, gang, gang.* It also did something else that was quite funny. When it was banging its cymbals if you tapped it on the head and said 'stop it', it curled back its top and bottom lips and said, *aaark arrk arrk gang gang gang.* It was really very funny. Charlie loved it, and chortled and banged it on the head, 'stop it'; *aaark aaark aaark.* It was an expensive bit of fun, and as is usual with expensive bits of fun, we soon tired of it.

So, you see why I was more than surprised to be woken in the middle of the night with the noise of that toy monkey screaming away, *aaark aaark aaark.* Was it a burglar who had accidentally switched it on? Or was it Bootsie the cat playing with it? I wouldn't put it past Bootsie as he was a very clever cat. I switched the lights on and went into the sitting room. The monkey stared at me with its barmy, brown glass eyes. There was no-one in the room. Had I imagined it? I went back to bed and turned the lights off and soon fell off to sleep. Then came the dawn and, *aaark arrk aaark.* There it was again. I was out of bed in a tick but whoever was playing with that silly monkey was quicker than I for the monkey sat alone and silent, its lips curled back and cymbals held out straight. Now what was going on? And another thing, where was Bootsie?

I soon found out. He was sitting in the middle of Eileen's bedroom in that patient posture that cats adopt when they are waiting for something to come out of somewhere with his front feet tucked underneath his chest, head pointing towards the dressing table. Eileen was sitting up in bed perhaps a little tense.

'There is somebody in this room', she said.

'You're dead right and whatever it is, is under the dressing table'. Bootsie was pointing that way.

By bending down I could see what it was under the dressing table. It was the biggest stoat that I have ever seen. A most beautiful stoat lying motionless. Was it dead? I put out a hand to pick it up, *aaark aaark.* It wasn't the monkey, it was the stoat and it was far from being dead.

Now a stoat is not a large animal but is most astonishingly fierce. Move your hand anywhere near it and, *arrk aark aaark*; that noise is calculated to make you jump a yard in the air. So, how do you catch a stoat? To try to do so with bare hands is sheer madness as you would be bitten to ribbons. I went to get a pair of gloves, and when I returned Bootsie had moved through about 45 degrees and was pointing at the chest of drawers. So thats where the stoat had moved to. I moved the chest, *ark aaark*. Quick as a flash, it darted — it was too quick for me.

Bootsie, like a weather vane in a changing wind, had swung around and was pointing towards the whatnot in the corner. He turned his head up a looked at me. 'There you are old man, he's under the whatnot, go on — get him'. I could see the stoat's quick little face sticking out from underneath the whatnot. Bootsie was doing nothing about catching the stoat. He appreciated only too well the full potential of that ferocious animal. A frontal attack was pure madness he knew he would be torn to bits. So how did he catch him in the first place? I believe he caught the stoat unawares, pounced on him and got him by the back of the neck. Well he is a most clever cat. The stoat, feeling himself caught by the neck, immediately gave up and went all soft and limp for stoats too, are most clever animals and it's reasoning must have been thus 'I'm caught by the neck and whoever has caught me will sooner or later have to put me down: there is nothing I can do to save myself but go soft and limp'. And so he stayed limp and lifeless while Bootsie brought him, swinging from side to side, up the garden through the cat flap and oh yes, along to Eileen's bedroom, and there he let him go saying, 'Mum I've brought you a smashing bit of ermine'.

Now, Bootsie was hoping to play with the stoat in the same way that he likes to play with a mouse. But he quickly realised that a stoat is not a mouse after he heard those warning screams *aaark aaark aaark*. A stoat, like many other animals, would prefer to give out a warning rather than fight. It was then that I realised that it was foolish to think of even trying to catch him. He was in full possession of all his faculties, Bootsie had not damaged him at all and, unlike a trapped bird, he did not lose his head. I could see by the way he looked towards the windows that if he could find his own way out he would soon go. I opened all the doors, back and front, and chivvied the stoat with a walking stick; away he went like a flash. The french

windows were wide open but Bootsie had beaten him to it and was waiting for him. It was a magnificent confrontation. To see these two very clever animals, both of them fully aware of each other's potential. Bootsie with one paw up saying, 'I could smack you down if I wanted to', and the stoat replying, through his little curled lips, 'you touch me and I'll bite your nose off, *aaark aark arrk*. And away it went down the garden.

Bootsie was much faster than the stoat but he deliberately cantered slowly behind, making no attempt to catch it. It was one of the prettiest things you ever did see. They both disappeared into the field at the bottom of the garden. Bootsie was soon back. He'd had a pretty good morning really. There are not that many cats who can catch and bring in a live stoat. He sat there, cleaning between his toes, looking absolutely confident and very beautiful. Just for fun, I give the toy monkey a whirl. *Gang gang gang,* 'stop it' *aaark arrak*. Bootsie wasn't fooled. He turned a tired eye on me. He knew the difference between a toy monkey and a captive stoat. He is a clever little cat. Well they all are, the stoat, the monkey and Bootsie. Three clever little monkeys.

Mind how you go

Animals that live in zoos and have been messed about a bit by human-beings, quickly develop their own funny little ways. But some of them are not so funny. Most animals in the wild will do their best to keep out of the way of homo sapiens and will have nothing to do with them. But supposing that they can't get out of the way and are cornered, then look out, they could attack. Of course, if Zoos animals are cornered, enclosed and unable to get out of the way, should you venture into their enclosures you stand a good chance of getting a four penny one. So you have got to be careful because you cannot tell just by looking at an animal how it is going to behave.

Now zoo keepers are generally most considerate people. They will tell you exactly what the character of any animal is like, in which you show an interest. 'No, you can't do anything with her she will kill you. Now he's lovely: give him a bit of apple and he's your friend for life'.

It isn't only the large animals that can do you a mischief in fact, they can be quite tiny. There was a little marmoset at Jersey Zoo that weighed only an ounce or two, and yet he put more people in hospital than any other animal in the zoo. He was a dear little thing to look at and encouraged exclamations of. 'Oh isn't he lovely. Come on then'. And then that dear member of the public, in spite of all the warning notices, would lean over and put a finger through the mesh so that they could stroke the little darling. Bang, he would have them got you. A horrible bite from a dear little darling. The keeper would have told them what to expect if he had been asked. And so, as a sort of travelling keeper, I will never go into an enclosure until I have had a chat with the local keeper and learn about his animals' funny little ways.

When I went to the Zoo at Copenhagen and met the boss there who was very quick to tell me of the wonderful, friendly animals that were there.

'Oh, we have two young tigers and you can doing anything what you want wiz zem. Zey are marvellous, zey are quite big but zey still have a bottle of warm milk each in the afternoon. You like to go in with zem this afternoon'.

'Yes, love to' I replied.

He picked up the phone and gabbled away in Danish. 'Right, half past two. Now we are having some elephants. Zey walk around the zoo holding tails you know. Zere are four of zem and you can riding on the leading elephant. You like to do this?'

'Yes love to'.

He picked up the phone again and gabbled away in Danish. 'Good half-past four. Good. Now I have to go away for two days but Hans is coming to show you where are the tigers and the elephants'.

Well Hans did come and I could see that he was not a very happy man, in fact, he was a most dreadful character, and walked with the heavy tread of impending doom. But I put it down to the long dark winters and off we went with a Danish camera team to where the tigers lived. Hans spoke no English, French or German, neither did the keeper of the tigers. I could see the tigers in the background. They were young but big. [Mind you with the passing of the years, those tigers seem to get bigger and bigger as my memory stretches back — but for tiger cubs who still had a bottle of milk they were big.] The tiger keeper had two plastic bottles of warm milk ready for me. It had all been very efficiently arranged. I will never forget the look on the keeper's face as he handed me the two warm plastic bottles. He had got rather a skull-like head and was wearing a strange grin: a fixed glazed grin. He reminded me of a living death's head with a cap on. And beside him, the mournful Hans looking like a Victorian undertaker.

I should have recognised a couple of very bad omens when I saw them but I didn't and went into the tigers' enclosure with a plastic bottle of warm milk in each jacket pocket. The tigers were absolutely delighted to see me. They said, '*haaa haaa, heres a bit of fun haaa*'. I was a bit of fun alright for in a split second I had got a tiger on my back. He hung from my shoulders with the talons deep into the shoulder padding of the jacket but the padding and the jacket could not support him. He started to slip down ripping the jacket as he went. It was when his face was level with my right buttock that he decided to take a bite but it was just a bit too much for him.

This was very much like an experience that a friend of mine had in a railway train. Sitting opposite to him was an old man who had not a tooth in his head. This was very plain to see as the old man had a bag of very firm big tomatoes. He wanted to eat his tomatoes but his old leather gums could make no impression on the tough red orbs. After several attempts, and a lot of sloshing noises, the tough tomato still had not been penetrated and the old man in desperation held out this tomato and said, 'Excuse me do you think you could start this tomato for me'. Do you think you could start this tomato for me? The tiger on my back was in the same predicament as the old man in the train he really needed someone to start my right buttock for him. I felt he teeth gouging away. The blood running down my leg. I later realised it wasn't blood running dowm my leg but warm milk from the torn plastic bottles. Certainly, they were only playing but it was extremely rough playing when you finish up with your jacket in shreds and the seat of your trousers well and truly out. I learnt a little later that the tiger keeper had not been in with those tigers for six weeks as he considered them to be too dangerous.

I was lucky to get out so lightly with the tigers, still, you need a little luck when there's death and an undertaker around. But now of course I was pushing my luck. I knew this when I saw the four elephants. Alright perhaps they did walk around the zoo holding tails but they hadn't done it for months, as far as I could see. They were restless, irritable and not really in control. It took about a half-an-hour to get the leading elephant to kneel down so that I could get on her back or more correctly, her neck. I remember seeing Hans gaze sadly and wistfully at the sky.

Now I don't know if you have ever ridden an elephant but

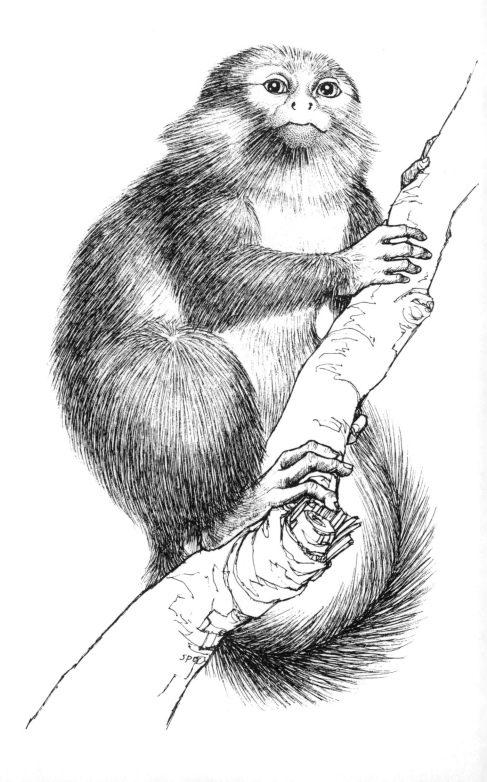

its rather like sitting on the edge of a moving cliff and not at all like riding a horse, where you do have reins and a long neck in front of you which you can cling to in case of difficulties. On an elephant there is nothing. Not only that, but the elephant's shoulder blades or, whatever it is, very powerfully prods you in the seat, first one side then the other.

To make matters worse, the elephant on which I was sitting kept putting her trunk right up and back smelling me all over. She didn't like what she smelt at all. 'It was wasn't it, *sniff sniff,* yes, *sniff sniff,* yes yes, *sniff sniff* Tiger! Tiger!' And off she went out of control. The keepers started to shout and scream. But she was going flat out and I could feel those pistons banging me in my seat. *Boom boom boom boom.* Hans ran in front of us waving his arms. *Boom boom boom boom.* Hans couldn't stop her. He ran off towards the zoo office, going to phone for an ambulance, no doubt, *boom boom boom boom* he continued on. There is a large area of lawn at Copenhagen Zoo, acres and acres of glorious green. We crossed it in about eight seconds — well nearly crossed it when I realised just what my elephant was going to do. She was heading for the avenue of trees with the low branches. She was going to get me off her back in no uncertain manner. Elephants are far from being daft. *Boom boom boom boom.* Bang — I went flying through the air and landed on my back, and for a few seconds the air was full of elephants' feet. I was lucky once again.

But it doesn't pay to push your luck. That is why you need to be well informed about the character of the animal you are about to tangle with. Because Zoo animals develop their own funny little ways. Some of them, not so funny.

Plonky the parrot

I became an anthropomorph at a very early age. It is hardly to be wondered at as my father was a natural anthropomorph. He absolutely accepted the fact that animals experienced much the same emotions and feelings as human beings. He always suggested to me what the thoughts of our cat were: sometimes they were not very much, or sometimes he suggested what the cat was going to do next. In other words how to 'read' an animal's mind because when you grow up and have to deal with our dear, dumb friends, it is essential that you are able, more or less, to predict what they are going to do next.

All good cattlemen, cowmen, shepherds, and horsemen can read their animal friends up to a point. You do not need scientific training, or have to go on courses, to be able to spot in a tick that the highly nervous strawberry-roan heifer that you are driving down the lane with 30 other heifers is about to jump the hedge. You will hear the cowman say in a well modulated voice: 'hold back all hold back all, 'ers thinking of jumping' and you can indeed, see that 'er is thinking of jumping. That wild eye, that raised head, the desperate looking around searching for a low place, or a weak place, in the hedge through which to half jump or half lunge.

Cows and heifers are not designed to jump and a heifer who jumps or tries to jump, a fence or a hedge usually ends up with an injury of some sort. Barbed wire is brutal stuff and hawthorn hedges will cut and scratch.

'Hold back all, hold back all, 'ers thinking of jumping'. And so as 'er is thinking of jumping the best thing, for a start at least, is to hold back. Slow down, take the pressure off the herd you are driving and stop chivving them on too much as if she is thinking of jumping and does jump then everyone is going to have one heck of a time. Well, if its the first time that 'er has jumped she will surely make a mess of it. By taking off the pressure, the herd spreads down the lane and 'er that's been thinking of jumping, feels calmer, not pursued and therefore doesn't jump. There is no known Highway code book with the rules of cattle driving, you have just got to be a bit of an anthropomorph. And so I became one at a very early age.

Being able to read animals' minds stood me in good stead early on as we had a talking parrot. He was an African grey; he talked to me and I talked to him. He was as close to a human being as any animal I had ever met in my life. That is why one morning in London, during the blitz, I chanced upon a pet shop. Now quite a lot of us remember the blitz and the noise it made and for those who don't remember the bombs, will have heard enough recordings of the bombs making their eerie sound, *pheee pheee pheee.* The blitz had been very bad that night and the pet shop was almost empty save for one dear African grey all alone in his cage. He'd had a terrible couple of weeks with not a wink of sleep and deep grey lines had appeared under his eyes. He beaked and clawed his way round the cage in a lost dreamlike way. He was demented. I bought him and asked that he be put on the train to our little country station on a branch line in Wiltshire.

Do you know even in the middle of the war, with the bombs peppering all over the place, those old steam trains pulled their loads of merchandise and people all over the British Isles. They never seemed to falter.

Therefore I was a bit surprised when I went to our little, old branch line railway station to pick up my African grey only to find out that he hadn't turned up. He should have changed at Swindon but instead had gone on down to Taunton and had to be re-directed. The old station master and I didn't know that so I asked him to give me a ring when my parrot showed up.

'That's alright my old dear, I'll ring 'ee as soon as ee gets ere. Whats er look like?' the station master enquired.

Well he'll be in a largish cage and the cage will be covered in sacking and stitched up'. I answered.

'Ar, alright my old dear', replied the pleasant, rosy-apple station master.

That is why some hours later I was a bit upset when he was

on the phone in a bit of a temper.

'That you?'

'Yes'.

'Ere, that blinking bird of yours has turned up'.

'Oh good'.

'No 't'int good, you come and get him at once'.

Worriedly I asked 'What, has he got out?'

'No he hasn't got out but you come and get him straight away'.

'Well what the matter', I persisted.

'Never mind what's the matter you come and get him and be quick about it,.

This anger was unusual coming from our dear rosy-apple station master. I buzzed off to the station and there was the dear old man in his thread-bare office, with just one black lump of coal in the fire place threatening to errupt sometime next week.

'Whatever is the matter?'

'Whatevers the matter, huh!' he angrily repeated.

There was the cage in the middle of the office covered in sacking and neatly stitched up.

Our dear rosy-apple station master demanded, 'you get him out of 'ere 'cos I can't stand it.

'Can't stand what?'

And then the bird under the sacking did it, he went *pheee pheeee pheee.* He had copied the noise that had driven him to the demented state in which I had found him in that London pet shop during the blitz.

Now even in the country we were fairly familiar with the sound of bombs. German planes that were lost and off course often just let the whole lot of bombs go; so every one recognised that dreaded sound. The trouble was that in the country there was no air raid warning to put you on your metal. Suddenly out of the blue to hear *pheee pheee pheee.* That is all my African grey ever did say, save for the stock parrot noises, *cluck cluck,* and the parrot pentatonic scale, *whistle Whistle.*

I don't know why but perhaps you may have noticed, that parrots always seems to whistle a pentatonic scale. Now I cannot imagine that parrot owners go round teaching their parrots the pentatonic scale, so can only assume that parrots, having learnt from us how to whistle, have an inclination towards composition and established their own avant garde pentatonic school. Whistle — that is all that dear parrot, whom we called Plonky, ever did. Until one day when he was getting over his shell shock state he said in a very slurred drunken way. 'Do you want a drink? Do you want a drink?'

Like most African greys, dear Plonky was most affectionate to those whom he got to know but when strangers were about, he would poise on one foot, turn his head slightly sideways and just listen to what was going on, not making a sound save to rustle his feathers and puff them out at bit.

Sometimes friends from London would come to spend the week end in the country to get away from the bombs. After dinner they would stretch out and relax in front of a comforting open fire. All was peace, perfect peace. Plonky would let them settle down for about ten minutes and then he would do it, *pheee pheee pheee.* The guests would dive for cover and after they realised that they were alone under the table, they would come out quite bewildered but very definitely shaken. It was then that Plonky would say, 'do you want a drink?' They most certainly did.

Now I sometimes thought that Plonky might be getting his own back on the human race for making his life in the pet shop such a hell, dropping bombs around him night after night. But that is going a bit far. The first time he did it must have been by accident but having done it once, every other time he did it was perfectly timed, knowing full well the effect it would have. He never failed to produce that effect. So if being anthropomorphic means putting human connotations on the animal behaviour, I wonder what the reverse would be. Like animals putting animal connotations on human behaviour? If there is such a word it can't be a very nice one.

Over the permitted level

There are those who say that although some of us may be able to 'read' animals, that is, predict what they are going to do, there are not many animals capable of being able to 'read' us. Well that's fairly understandable as many of us are unable to read ourselves. Consider for a moment or two the large number of poor maladjusted souls that flake out once a week, sometimes more, on the couch of their own special shrink. There, they cosily indulge in themselves and slobber through their early childhood like the hot buttered toast they were coddled on. What went wrong? Did your nanny spoil you? Did your father rule with a rod of iron? Did you discover your mother in the potting shed misbehaving with the young gardener? Well, these things do make a difference you know by permanently affecting you. And the permutations of things that go right for you, and those that go wrong for you, stretch from birth to death. Sad isn't it? So if we don't understand ourselves, how can animals possibly try to analyse us in the same way as we try to analyse ourselves and other animals? I think not but we must not throw that suggestion out of the window without probing about just a bit.

Care to drift back to the turn of the century when there were more horses resident in this country than human beings. They did a lot of our work for us. They helped to grow our crops and then hauled them about. They carried us on their backs and in our carts and carriages. There were millions of horses about and thousands of them had problems. My mother always enquired into the character of every horse that was going to transport her about. Well, some were frightened of flying paper while some were frightened of whistling steam trains. Some horses kicked, some bit, some bolted. Indeed some horses wouldn't go backwards while some hated going forwards. Horses have days when they are just awkward and days when they aren't. Why? Horse analysis was always a pretty good talking point and the diagnosis was usually bad treatment which included thrashing, and a dreadful assortment of very inventive but thoroughly sadistic practices. Prognosis — Knackers Yard.

However, sometimes animal analysis is tackled in a rather reckless way. I once spent a day acting as keeper to Chi-Chi, the giant panda at London Zoo. My fellow keepers were most helpful and told me that when I went in with Chi-Chi to, 'watch it because at times she could be funny'. Well, of course, when a giant Panda's funny, it isn't really a bit funny. And as we know precious little about giant Pandas, and as I knew even less than that I found it an extremely difficult animal to 'read'. How would I know when it was going to be funny? You couldn't tell whether it was going to come over to you and give you a kiss and a cuddle or slash you to tatters, for a giant Panda's face is rather like a masked burglar and tells you nothing. A keeper came in with me just in case Chi-Chi turned funny. I also took with me a large bouquet of bamboo shoots.

'You can't get too near her because she knows you're different. She'll take a swipe at you' said my mate. 'Just stretch your arm out with the bamboo'.

I stretched my arm out and Chi-Chi started to pick and nibble at the bamboo shoots. I moved in closer, and closer, until I was right in front of her. I gazed into her mysterious eyes. I didn't think she was going to be funny and she wasn't. I went back to my mate when Chi-Chi had finished my bamboo bouquet.

'That's funny you know, that's dead funny, I can never get that close to her she always takes a swipe at me'. He sounded amazed.

'Does she?' I replied nervously.

'Yes, wonder what it is, wonder what it is? Well, you're wearing the same uniform but she knows you're different. Mmmm, I've got it, I've got it'.

'What?'

'You're wearing brown boots. We all wear black boots but you're wearing brown boots: that's it she likes brown

boots, brown boots'.

My fellow keeper had made a snap analysis. If we explored a little further we would ask what had black boots done to Chi-Chi that Chi-Chi didn't like? Perhaps we can go no further save to say that should you meet a giant panda on a lonesome road make sure you are wearing your brown boots.

The one thing that stuck in my mind was that my fellow keeper said that Chi-Chi knew I was different. If he was right then I must have been nicely different and not nastily different for some animals can find you nastily different. This was brought home to me by some Bactrian camels that lived at Marwell Zoological Park. At school we were told that a camel was a beast of burden and, being a beast of burden, it was pretty well doomed. Now having been classified by us as a beast of burden, it somehow gave us the right to bung five hundredweight of whatever we liked on its back, and prod it from here to Samarkand. 'Well, it was the camel's own fault why they were a beast of burden, so they must jolly well get on with it'. But we can hardly blame camels for looking as they do. They have been taken advantage of and been put upon. The Marwell camels looked like they knew that they had been put upon for all this time but in fact, they are very charming, gentle and extremely polite. The only danger with polite camels is that sometimes they do get skittish. Rather like the stage chamber maid who has been slyly pinched on the rear by the master. They will suddenly go, '*woohoo,* Oh! you are a one'. The camels leap in the air and kick their legs out and gallop about not looking where they are going. That's the danger — to be blundered into. To be blundered into by a camel hurts a good deal. If you are blundered into by three camels at the same time that could mean a quick call for the ambulance. If the camels are in skittish mood, you just do not exist.

On this particular morning the Marwell camels were on their best behaviour. It was during the spring and the camels were shedding their winter coats. They looked a mess. Lumps of moulting hair hanging from their flanks and humps like moth-eaten tatty second-hand rugs. They always look self-conscious at this time rather like a housewife caught at lunchtime still in her curlers. 'Oh don't, look at me I look a dreadful fright'. The camels came over to inspect me as I walked into their enclosure. The idea was to film the camels in their moulting condition and to help them get rid of their old hair which they can only do by rubbing. Obviously they like having that itchy old hair rubbed away. I talked to them very softly and pulled away the loose hair. They talked to me, and each other, and I knew that our cameraman was getting some good pictures. We weren't recording any sound as microphones and booms get in the way and, quite frankly, are just a nuisance. It is far better to put the commentary and sound effects on later. We got a fine sequence with the Bactrian camels and after thanking them for being so helpful, we went off to lunch.

It was during lunch that a telephone call came to ask us if we could film a one minute trailer for the forthcoming programmes. What better location than with those most agreeable camels! We would have to use sound, of course, as the organisers wanted a 'Piece to Camera'. We set up the equipment and I walked into the camel enclosure. The camels came over to greet me and I started to talk to the camera. Naturally, I had to raise my voice. And then it happened. The camel of my left suddenly let out a great *woosh* and I was hit in the face with a gobbet of chewed tobacco, or so it seemed. Then the camel on my right did exactly the same thing. They were spitting, and camel spit is not very nice stuff. They kept on spitting at me and then shoving me so that I had to get out of the enclosure where the camera crew were rolling about on the ground with laughter.

Now why had the camels so suddenly changed their nature and become different characters? They hadn't but I had. I was different. How? Well, I was still wearing the same clothes because should I have changed clothes then I would certainly have been different. No it wasn't the clothes but my voice was different. I was no longer talking softly but loudly and it could have been that that made me different.

70

I often think that camels are perhaps the only animals that could be fooled by that Mozart opera Cosi fan tutte, where two husbands dress up and their wives do not recognise them. Camels would believe that: no-one else would.

When the rot sets in

One of the more dubious aspects of this permissive society is that we are now privileged to see and hear things that we have never seen or heard before. Well perhaps not heard before as when we were very young all, or most, of the wicked words of this wicked world, simply flew towards us like iron filings to a magnet. At the age of about eight, I had gathered a collection of swear words — for that is what they were called — and these words put me on an equal footing with a dockside stevedore and a cattle drover. In that respect, I became an adult long before I was ten years old. Ah, but to be in possession of these horrible words put you in a very dangerous position. These forbidden words were like the devil himself and they had the quality of mercury. If one slipped out across that impulsive little tongue to explode with a flash and a puff of black smoke in the playground: then you were for it. Even a petulant little 'damn' could fetch you a thundering clout around the earhole. It was one thing knowing the words but it was quite another thing saying them. All the little boys in my class at school knew these words, and such was the enormity of the crime in saying them aloud that even your dearest friend would inform upon you.

'Sir, Morris has just said Bloody Hell'

'I couldn't help it Sir, I made a blot on my arithmetic book'. And then we would both get walloped. Dearest friend for repeating what I had said and, yours truly, for starting the ball rolling as it were. To make matters worse, we were then kept behind after school.

Many years later I wasn't at all surprised when I heard that in Nazi Germany children informed on their parents for expressing the honest opinions about Hitler, Goering and Goebbels. They were telling on their parents and the satisfying thing about sneaking or informing is that it is a miserable way of getting your own back but at the same time bestowing upon yourself a shabby mantle of piety. You could get done to death for just saying things in exactly the same way that we got walloped for saying those awful words. But switch on the television nowadays and within the hour you will hear many of those once forbidden words which, had I used them with such regularity as a child, would have earned me a thrashing and expulsion from school forever. So perhaps they weren't all that bad. When it comes to things that we are asked to look at, then things have taken a turn perhaps not for the worse but certainly not for the better.

Many people fix the blame, or the turning point, as to what is now permissible on the judgement given over the book, Lady Chatterley's Lover. They claim that this was when the rot set in. Well that may be so but consider some of the past and present Natural History films as they have got quite a lot to answer for. Now they say that the camera does not lie. True, but the director and the film editor can mislead the viewer by presenting a picture that has been manipulated, which shows what is a very rare occurrence as something that happens twenty-four hours a day. On several occasions I have been to Africa to look at the wildlife there. I have seen lions and yes, I have seen buffalo, but I have never seen a lion kill a buffalo. I have seen hyenas and wildebeeste but I have never seen hyenas take on a young wildebeeste. You have got to be hanging about for a considerable time with a very long lens to see these sort of happenings. But film them and string them all together: cheetahs killing gazelles, eagles killing birds, crocodiles eating deer, and you can present a continuous picture of a very bloody African wildlife indeed. And so it is but most of the time all is peace and quiet to the naked human eye.

Some years ago we were watching television when some friends called in unexpectedly to see us. They were a gentle couple, Mr. and Mrs. Bland, both very respectable, reasonable people.

'Ah! How very nice to see you'.

'We are not interrupting you are we?'

'No, just looking at the telly'.

'Oh, it looks interesting please don't turn it off'.

'Well I wouldn't mind just seeing it, as it only has a few more minutes to run'.

Mr. and Mrs. Bland settled themselves down to watch a film about Natural History. There on the television screen appeared a kestrel, hovering, and then a heron flying one flap a second or thereabouts, beautifully held in the middle of the frame by one of those marvellous cameramen. The commentator then said something like, 'and now the autumn air vibrates with the roar of the fallow deer. It is the time of the rut'.

Now like the killing of buffalo, the slaughter of wildebeeste, gazelles and deer, I have never seen a rut save through the courtesy of a thumping great telescopic lens, even though I live where deer are very thick on the ground you still hardly ever even see one. Mr. and Mrs. Bland were the sort of people who had probably never seen a deer in their lives.

On the screen appeared a fine shot of a stag roaring his head off. Something would be happening soon. The commentator had now assumed the hallowed tones of a curate at evensong. 'The stags have no time to feed or sleep during the rut' Mrs. Bland was a bit unsure of this statement and for her own benefit said out loud 'What's the rut?'

Mr. Bland who was a bit of a wag said, 'you and I have been in one for years dear, but not this sort, Hahahaha'.

Mrs. Bland was getting most uneasy as two stags with a rattle that sounded like someone tipping a load of logs, crashed their antlers together and started shoving and snorting.

'What are they doing?' asked Mrs. Bland.

'Fighting dear', replied her husband.

'Whatever for?'

Poor Mrs. Bland: she could not accept that nature in the raw is seldom mild and could not fully appreciate the anxiety and violence of the rut. The lady deer, the hinds, continued to graze away as though nothing was happening. Every now and again, one of them would look up to where the stags were staggering and bashing about doubtlessly hoping that perhaps

Stag Stephen would lick the pants off Stag Harold as he was a much more refined looking character. As it happened, Stag Harold shoved Stag Stephen to the point of no return, and Stephen trotted off in defeat, swearing and blowing-off steam.

Now, while all this was going on, a couple of young bucks had slipped in and were chatting-up a couple of very attractive young hinds. Stag Harold must have had his suspicions for he spotted them at once. With a thundering roar he was after them and drove them off stage right just as Stag Edward moved in stage left. The whole sequence was very much like a French farce and, like a French farce, the skirmishing so far was only suggestive.

The delightful aspect of a French farce is that everyone understands the manoeuvrings of the characters involved and are tickled to death by the frustrations, deceit, double dealing and sheer naughtiness of the cast. Scene one: the master is heard in the hall outside. He has given himself away because he pinches the parlourmaid's behind and she goes, *Woo hoo*. This warns the mistress of the house in the drawingroom who is with her fancy boyfriend. He hops it, of course, out of the french windows, and she fans the air to try to get rid of his cigar smoke. The master enters. 'Sniff sniff what's this, cigar smoke?' 'Oh no, er . . .'. The master nips smartly out through the French windows into the garden to search about in the bushes. The fancy boyfriend appears in the hallway and slips into the drawingroom to steal a kiss from the missus; he then tiptoes out of a side door. And that's about as far as we get with the French farce situation and everybody is giggling away with glee. But with the rut, as they say, it goes the whole hog. As Mr. and Mrs. Bland were finding out.

The commentator drops his voice to a sanctimonious whisper and says, 'And now copulation takes place'. As though we didn't know!

Mrs. Bland was terribly shocked and exclaimed 'Oh No!' Mr. Bland looks thoughtfully at his finger nails, then at his wrist-watch, and turned his gaze to the ceiling, no doubt recollecting the dear dead days.

As I say, this was many years ago and it left us all in a state of embarrassed shock as we had never before seen what happens after the final curtain falls in a French farce. We knew what happened but we had never seen it demonstrated in public on television before. Nowadays it seems a television play is not complete unless we are treated to a French farce going the whole hog, although we are spared the hushed whispers of the commentator saying 'And now copulation takes place' There are those who say that the rot set in with the trial over the book, Lady Chatterley's Lover. But I think the rot set in with the rut.

Slight embarrassments

No doubt you will recall the old radio programme, 'Have a Go' in which contestants were asked to describe their most embarrassing moment. It was supposed to produce simply excruciating stories and hysterical shrieks of laughter and sometimes it did; but very often it did not. The stories that usually received houls of laughter more often than others related to ladies being discovered in their knickers by total strangers. This scene was something that everybody understood. However, embarrassment is a matter of sensitivity and the measure of your embarrassment depends as they say, in the thickness of your skin. I know people who have never been embarrassed in their lives and others who are in an almost permanent state of embarrassment.

Some of our animal friends have learnt to embarrass us to a point of anger. For example, a rider who goes out to catch his horse in the paddock, five times out of six has no trouble at all. But on the sixth day, as he approaches, the horse just tosses its head, goes into a ballroom twirl and trots off to the other end of the paddock. It will do this ten or twenty times. Apples, lumps of sugar and carrots are just a joke. 'What makes you think I like that rubbish, *hehehe,* don't make me laugh'. And then for no apparent reason he suddenly allows himself to be caught and his halter put on. If one horse can sometimes be a problem, then two dogs can be a real headache.

I know two dogs that were more than a bit barmy. But then their owners were more than barmy. There is an old country saying that says, 'two dogs are worse that one dog ever knew how to be? That certainly applied to these two dogs. If they ever got out on their own they would create havoc. Shut up in the house they were still barmy but fairly harmless. One winter's evening there was a small dinner party at the house. When the guests arrived, their overcoats were collected and laid out on a large bed upstairs. It was a good, jolly party and a

rattling good time was had by one and all. Time to leave, and the host went upstairs to collect the coats, only to find that the dogs were lying on the coats. And, they were eating the only fur coat in the collection. In fact, they were just a few mouthfuls short of finishing it. All that remained was a ripped and ragged lining and a few powder puffs of grey fur. Of course, that was an embarrassment of a different sort as those barmy dogs did not know what they were doing. Orang-utans on the other hand, know exactly what they are doing and, in my opinion, they are the most subtle of the great apes and can embarrass you with an ease of style that is almost lyrical.

There lived at Bristol Zoo an incredible orang called Jack. He was enormous, and when I first met him he was about fifteen years old, yet he was perfectly tame. Well, perhaps not perfectly tame because he was just being obedient. He was obedient to his keeper a certain Stanley Puddy. Jack was dominated by his keeper, Stanley. Stanley was the boss. Although Jack had long since become a mature adult he had not developed those great leather cheek flaps and that flabby chest balloon that marks the dominant male. When I first saw Jack I must say he did give me quite a shock. He could walk upright and often behaved rather like a tired old waiter whose feet have been giving him hell for years. Standing upright he presented a terrifying aspect. He was over five feet six tall and almost as wide, absolutely covered in what must have been a hundredweight of matted ginger wool which hung to the ground. Looking out of the top of this moving mountain of ginger wool you could see his crafty Bill Sykes face: thinking, watching, scheming, brooding.

On several occasions Stanley brought Jack to the television studios. Oh no, not in a cage. They walked into the studio hand in hand. Jack, had he wished, could have without too much trouble killed everybody in the studio. But he was as good as gold for he was obedient and dominated. However, there was always that look on his face that murmured, 'one day I'm going to get you'. He often murmured to me, 'one day I'm going to get you'. Everybody at the studio was terrified of Jack when he walked in hand in hand with Stanley. Canteen ladies rushed screaming around the tables. Commissionaires clutched their desks, their knuckles white and lips trembling. Cameramen put their cameras into reverse and veered off down to the other end of the studio. Everyone thought that we were taking a great risk in allowing this yeti into the studio especially as the programme was always transmitted live. This happened fifteen years ago, perhaps more, and such a thing could not happen now for the regulations have been considerably tightened up.

Back home at Bristol Zoo, Jack spent a lot of time thinking and lounging in his enclosure. This enclosure was a beautiful Victorian affair made of curved cast iron bars, and trailing all over this charming old iron basketwork was a wonderful wisteria. Jack had his own special shelf high up under the wisteria and here he used to lie and think of all the people that he was going to 'Get one day'. There he brooded and plotted, this great ginger ape, as he sat among the delicate pale mauve wisteria blossom.

Every day at about noon, Stanley would go into Jack's beautiful lounge and say, 'come on down Jack it's time for our bit of dinner'. Jack obeyed at once. He came down from his high shelf and with his massive arms and muscular legs, he would lower himself down the cast iron bars and be at Stanley's side in a couple of seconds. He would then hold out his enormous left hand and Stanley would take it and they would both walk hand-in-hand along the broad terrace of Bristol Zoo. It was an astonishing sight to watch them strolling slowly past the lush flower beds and going into the keepers' restroom. Stanley had an armchair to himself and Jack also had an armchair to himself; there they sat and had their bit of dinner. Stanley had his sandwiches and Jack a banana, or two, and a couple of tomatoes. After their dinner, Stanley liked a pipe of tobacco. Jack also had his pipe that he always kept on the window sill. He never filled it or lit it but he just sat and thoughtfully sucked it. It was a perfect imitation of Stanley save, that every now and again, he would stretch up one gigantic arm and catch hold of the cold water pipe that ran across the ceiling through the restroom; gently he would pull it down into a neat loop and then push it back straight again. He liked to keep himself in trim. I watched this amazing performance many times, these two old mates having their bit of dinner.

One day I said to Stanley, 'do you think that Jack would have a bit of dinner with me. We would like to film it'. Stanley had no doubt at all that Jack would perform with me.

He did say though, 'if he gets saucy, fump him'.

The thought of having to give Jack a 'fumping' did stop me in my tracks. Suppose Jack 'fumped' me back. Fortunately Bristol Zoo and the Bristol Royal Infirmary are not too far apart.

'Is that a wise thing to do Stanley, fump him'.

'Oh you got to fump him sometimes, come and sit in this chair'.

I sat in Stanley's chair with Jack glowering opposite me, sucking his pipe. Almost immediately, Jack stretched out his great hand, which looked like a bunch of bananas, and grasped my hand. He drew my hand slowly towards his mouth. Jack then rolled back his lips showing me his truly dreadful teeth. He was going to bite me. I quickly 'fumped' him. It was like hitting a coconut. I was in agony but Jack dropped my hand at once and cowered. That clip around the earhole hadn't hurt him one little bit and I don't suppose that he would have bitten me in any case. Jack had simply been testing me, in the same way in which a child will often test a parent, to see if the parent is in control and still the boss. The 'fump' that I gave Jack was purely a psychological 'fump' to him but physical agony for me. However he had signalled that I was the boss and so I arranged with Stanley that we would film Jack and I first of all in his wisteria lounge and then along the terrace and finally in the keepers' restroom.

We chose a beautiful day and soon set up a camera outside Jack's residence. The sun was shining, the light was perfect, not a dark cloud in the sky; we could start right away. Stanley stood alongside the cameraman so that he would be close at

hand just in case Jack got very saucy and needed a bit more than a 'fump'. I took the key from Stanley and pushed it into the lock. Jack was lying up on his shelf. He heard the lock click and flicked a quick glance at me. He knew at once that I was not Stanley. However I went into Stanley's routine, 'come on down Jack, its time for our bit of dinner'.

Jack swung out onto the bars at once, his colossal hulk dropping down like an express lift. He finished up with his back to me, standing up on two legs, he turned and grabbed my outstretched hand. He was behaving in exactly the same way that he behaved with Stanley. He walked slowly, hand in hand, toward the gate and the camera. As we passed the camera Jack looked at me steadily in the eyes. I thought I detected a mild smirk around his rubber lips and I imagined that he said, 'everything alright then mate?' Everything alright then mate! For he knew jolly well what he had done. By then, I jolly well knew what he had done. When he slid down the bars of his cage, finishing up on all fours, before he turned to give me his hand, he had picked up from the floor a large lump of something quite disgusting, palmed it in his great hand and now I had got it jointly in the hand that I held him. He knew perfectly well that the commodity he had handed me was of acute embarrassment to human beings. He had carried out his threat. 'One day I'm going to get you'. He'd got me, but in a most surprising way.

I think it is worth mentioning that shortly after this charming little scene, Stanley left the Bristol Zoo to work elsewhere. The dominance that he held over Jack went with him. Almost at oncce, Jack grew his leathery cheek flaps and developed that flabby chest balloon that marks the dominant male. And it occurred to me that it must have been something of an embarrassment for Jack to have been an adult male and not have the trimmings of a dominant male. His character inevitably changed to match his truly terrifying appearance and no-one dared go near him.

85

Revelations

There are times when our animal friends lead us very beautifully up the garden path by so innocently deceiving us. Or could it be that we underestimate their ability to exploit a situation that they perhaps have not met before?

There is a story of some people who ran a boarding kennels and cattery. They were a most conscientious couple for they knew only too well the pernickity affectations of the dear doggies and moggies left with them by their caring owners whilst they went for a holiday.

'He always likes a saucer of tea at about eleven in the morning and just before we go to bed at night, but then he has a sweet biscuit at well. He loves his sweet biscuit at night. He'll bark and bark unless he gets his sweet biscuit at night'.

'She won't eat any of the tinned foods, turns up her nose at them. She loves fillet steak minced but it has to be fresh minced. If you leave it for an hour she wont touch it'.

So all the idiosyncrasies of these little darlings were listened to, noted down and if possible, adhered to. It came to pass that a married couple called at the kennels one day and asked if there was a vacancy for a mongrel dog for a fortnight. There was.

They asked, 'could we bring the dog's chair in?'

'Of course,' they were told. Owners were strongly encouraged to bring as many of the pets personal effects as possible: blanket, own feeding bowls, basket, rubber bone, slipper, lead and collar. Make the little fellow feel at home, not so much of a wrench'.

'Good,' and with that the happy owners trotted off.

On the day, the couple turned up with a horse box. This horse box was divided into two compartments and in the front compartment was the dog's chair. An enormous chair, a club armchair made about the turn of the century. A great wallowing chair that had lulled many a fifteen stone sozzled

managing director into a deep and rumbling sleep. The great mongrel that slept in this chair was shut away out of sight in the second compartment of the horse box. They had a terrible job to manhandle the chair into the reserved kennel. It wouldn't go unless they took the door off, so they took the door off. Some of the screws were rusted in but by jingo they did it. It took them over a half-an-hour to get that gargantuan chair in but again, by jingo, they did it. Then they put the door back on even though three off the screws were rusted and useless.

'Will the door hold him?' the owners were asked. 'Oh! yes that'll hold him we'll go and get him,' and in they went.

They came out carrying a sort of dwarf chihuahua with a touch of neurotic Jack Russell and a hint of twitchy toy poodle. Its overall appearance was that of a trembling rat but his owner's were passionately fond of him. In amazement, the owner's were asked, 'and that his chair?'

'Yes, they confirmed, 'thats Poppum's chair'.

'But isn't the chair a bit on the big side for Poppums?'

'Ah Poppums doesn't sleep in the chair, Poppums sleeps under the chair'.

So you see, Poppums was far from being daft. In that great chair he would be vulnerable when asleep but under the chair, anything bigger than a rat, just couldn't get at him. It was quite a revelation the way in which that pampered little mite had devised his own special survival technique. Poppums was what might be called a successful animal had he been able to find his own food. For the measure of a successful animal, of course, is that it is able to find its own food, defend itself, and produce young.

I once ran into a mob of the most successful animals on the island of Steep Holm. Steep Holm is an island dropped down in the Bristol Channel beside another island Flat Holm. In the spring, both of these islands are simply infested with sea gulls. Yes, they are infested because the gulls will simply not tolerate the presence of any other animal and they will attack it as they are defending their chicks. No matter how big the animal might be, if it poses a threat the gulls will attack like a squadron of

fighter planes. For this reason, it is good sense to wear one of those awful swollen yellow helmets the sort that building constructors wear. These helmets make you feel very big headed, but try walking bare-headed on Steep Holm in the spring time and you will find that one sharp bop on the head by a gull's beak, is like being hit with the sharp end of a toffee hammer. Multiply that forty times in a half-a-minute, and your eyes begin to water, there is a buzzing in your ears and you know, before long, that the woodpeckering that's going on will have penetrated into the frontal lobes and you'll be dulalay by the morrow. So it is best to wear a big headed helmet as it does save you from a hammering.

Now Steep Holm is rather a special island. Broadly speaking it is a Nature Reserve and is visited by appointment by bird watchers, botanists and the like. All well-behaved, public-spirited people who come to visit this now uninhabited island for the tranquillity and peace of mind, to observe and contemplate the wonders of nature. They are, if I may say so, a pretty decent class of people. So you see I was more than put out when I found a filthy plastic bag on the foot path. Not a big plastic bag I grant you — about eight or nine inches square —but there was another and another. The whole island seemed steeped in old, filthy plastic bags. Did the visitors come here with their sandwiches in plastic bags, wolf-up the bread and bloater paste, then just chuck the bags away — no it couldn't possibly be them. And then I found a gizzard. it looked like a chicken's gizzard and it was in a filthy, old plastic bag. But how did that get here? Were these naturalists a bit peculiar bringing raw chickens gizzards on a picnic?

It took a little time to work it out. Our affluent society was to blame. Our wasteful, throw-away, unnatural society had created a gizzard mountain. And where was this gizzard mountain? Not very far away. Within sight of Steep Holm lies the seaside resort of Weston-Super-Mare. There must be dozens of small hotels in Weston-Super-Mare that buy their chickens frozen and, neatly tucked inside the chicken, is a plastic bag full of giblets. Now although Mrs. Beeton paid a lot of attention to giblets, the hotel keepers of Weston-Super-Mare do not. Mrs. Beeton makes your mouth water with stewed giblets, giblet stuffing, giblet soup, giblet pie and, of course, one that should never be ignored, giblet gravy. But even if you do not wish to explore these delights, surely chicken liver risotto cannot be abandoned. Oh yes, apparently it can. The whole bagful of giblets is chucked out with the rubbish and it finds its way, along with thousands of other bags of giblets, to the Weston rubbish dump which becomes the central giblet collecting depot. What a turn up for the book. The seagulls never had it so good. There they flock screaming with glee at this free giblet take-away service. Take away? Fly-away service, all neatly wrapped, beautifully fresh and nicely thawed out. The gulls bring their fly away giblets over the Steep Holm and there they indulge themselves in great luxury. The luxuries that we once so carefully guarded and treated so delicately, we now throw away it would seem with disdain. Still the gulls do pretty well on it; they are thriving. If more food means more little gulls, then the gull population of Steep Holm can only increase as long as we go on bunging our giblets away. The sea gulls of Steep Holm have very neatly turned themselves into a worthy giblet disposal unit. Quite a revelation, and you cannot help admire them for their initiative. But of course, they are messing up Steep Holm, and as so often happens admiration turns sour, and the sea gulls become thoroughly disliked.

I suppose that one of our most painful experiences is when an honest true love turns sour. There was once a good farmer who lived in the West Country. He was a farmer who practised the good old fashioned husbandry. His fields were clean, his crops were heavy, and his stock were fit, fat and well. His house was neatly painted, the milking parlour was well washed and spotless, and in his stable proudly stood his pride and joy, a most handsome chestnut horse. This hunter stood at over 17 hands, and had no vices. He was kind and gentle, simple as a little child. But he was also as clever as a cat; never stumbling or falling. His wind was as good as a church organ, his legs were shining chestnut steel. He face was sincere and affectionate.

The farmer truly loved his horse and called him Colonel. He was forever taking him titbits, patting him, polishing him up and talking to him: talking and talking. He used to say as people often do, 'you know that Colonel he understands every word I say'. He was deeply in love with his horse.

One day, his young nephew came to stay for the week-end and he too, had one great love in his life, his motorcar. It was a vintage motorcar that he had discovered as a near wreck. He had bought it and spent several years restoring it in his spare time. Many missing or broken bits he made himself turning slender rods on his lathe, cutting cog wheels, filing tappits, grinding valves, rubbing, painting, spraying and polishing until the old car looked as smart and elegant as the day when it first emerged into the sunlight outside the factory. Well not exactly the same. It was an open-topped touring sports car with a folding canvas hood. Originally the hood had been black but the young nephew hoping to cut a bit of a dash with his magnificent car, spent hours finding a new impregnated canvas hood to suit his car. At last he found one — a lovely sheet of red canvas. The red was so startling that even if the car failed at attract attention the hood, without a doubt, would. And so he arrived driving his beautiful vintage, Grand Tourer, flushed with triumph and shining with pride. The farmer much admired the motor car and congratulated his nephew on a fine bit of restoration. A man after his own heart, thorough to a degree, workmanlike and stylish. But where to put it for the night?

Well, its not good to put it in any of the barns as they don't lock up, and that new cowman's kids are proper little devils. Into everything. Started one of the tractors last week, damn near smashed it up. No, put it somewhere where we can see it from the house'. The farmer thought then suggested, put it in that paddock there. All the main bedrooms look out over the paddock, so does the dining and sitting rooms. Yes that's the safest place, in the paddock.

The young nephew was rather shocked. 'But uncle there's a horse in that paddock'.

'A horse! a horse! You mean Colonel. Colonel wouldn't touch your car, course he wouldn't. What, that horse knows how to behave, don't you tell me he would harm that car he wouldn't. I've left combines out in that paddock, tractors, drills — all sorts. Never touched them. The idea. The idea'.

The farmer was really put out by the suggestion that his darling horse might get up to no good. They both went out into the paddock. It was summer time and The Colonel ambled over to greet them.

'You see', the farmer said, 'quiet as a lamb, lovely gentleman aren't you Colonel?' The Colonel nodded a modest acknowledgement and then walked with great dignity over to his favourite place in the paddock underneath an ash tree.

'You don't have to worry about Colonel, your little old car will be perfectly safe in here'.

And so the vintage car was driven into the paddock. The farmer and nephew went into the farm house for their supper of cold meat and pickles. After their supper they drank between them more than half a bottle of malt whisky, while the farmer went on at great length about the virtues of his beloved horse Colonel.

Thank goodness, he is still a comparatively young horse, many years of hunting left in him. Never get another one like him, never had one like him before'. And with tears in his eyes he poured out another good gulp of malt whisky and prayed to God that nothing would ever happen to the Colonel so that he would have to be put down. 'I could never bring myself to order it', he said as a single tear traced a trail over the farmer's wind-blown face. 'I could never bring myself to order it'.

They both went unsteadily to bed and as they parted on the landing the farmer said, 'if anything should happen to me you'll see to it that the Colonel gets a good home won't you. I think more of that horse than anything'.

Before climbing into his bed the nephew looked out of his window. A full moon was shining on the paddock. The Colonel was standing in his favourite place under the ash tree, at the other end of the paddock stood his beautiful vintage car with its startling red hood glowing in the moon light like the embers of a great fire. Came the dawn, as they say, and the nephew once again looked out of his window. The morning sun was shining strongly. The Colonel was still meditating quietly under the ash tree. And the beautiful vintage car — well — he couldn't believe it. The wondrous red hood of the car had gone. Yes gone. How absolutely awful, there must have been a gale. Surely there hadn't been a force ten gale in the night. He hadn't heard a thing. He dressed quickly and rattled downstairs, running out into the paddock to look at his car. No, there hadn't been a gale as the wooden struts of the hood were firmly in place, but fluttering here and there from the struts, were little pennants of tatters of the red canvas. His lovely red hood had been ripped away bit by bit. How? And then he saw something on the ground that made him realise that his hood had been eaten away, mouthful my mouthful. By this time the farmer had come down to breakfast and the nephew went back indoors.

'That horse' he said to the farmer, 'has eaten the hood of my car'.

Any malt whisky hang-over that the farmer may have had clouding his brain left him in a flash. 'What horse? What horse?'

'The Colonel has eaten my roof'.

For a moment it looked as though the farmer was going to strike his nephew down to the ground. 'How dare you say a thing like that, how dare you. The Colonel wouldn't do a thing like that, 'course he wouldn't, he wouldn't do a thing like that. Its that new cowman's kids the little devils, they done it they've done it'.

'I don't think so Uncle come and have a look'.

They both went out into the paddock. The Colonel always left his favourite place to come over and greet the farmer but this morning he stayed underneath the ash tree, as the pair went over to the car. The ragged flags of red canvas fluttered in the breeze. The farmer examined the remains of the hood.

'Yes, its those damned kids' declared the farmer.

'Thats what's done it, those kids,.

'I don't think so Uncle, look'. And he pointed out to his uncle something that he had already noticed near the car. It was the droppings of a horse, and woven neatly through all the droppings, were layers and layers of red canvas.

The farmer stared and stared at the red flecked droppings. Then slowly his incredulous gaze travelled across the grass to the horse standing under the ash tree. The light of his life, the apple of his eye, his Colonel. His Colonel stood there, so handsome and so dignified. The farmer stared and stared at him, then said in an awful stage whisper that had a hint of a death rattle in it, 'oooaaaaaa . . . The ghastly bugger'. Now that was a relevation!

Very much like you and me

It must have been said by millions of people, millions of times, that peoples' pets gradually become like the people that own them. Should that theory by contested, then millions will doubtless say that the opposite is true and that people become like the pets they own. Well, of course, both statements are exaggerations but somewhere along the line the comparisons between man and beast are so obvious that you have to look in the mirror to reassure yourself that you are indeed you and that you don't have a face like that saucy pig that has just winked at you.

Oh yes, I once knew a pig who used to tip its head to one side and wink, and seemed to be saying 'Wotcher cock'. 'You and I understand each other don't we mate. 'Course we do. All these others in this 'ere sty are a bit fick aren't they mate just a bit fick'.

Well he certainly didn't seem to be a bit 'fick', and when you are dealing with lots of pigs you will meet many that are like him. Its worth remembering that in the eighteenth century, pigs were used as gundogs. They were better at pointing and retrieving and were extremely soft in the mouth. Unfortunately, or perhaps fortunately, unlike dogs they were reluctant to obey commands, and if they felt like a good, muddy, wallow they would have one, rather than go out shooting. This clearly shows that pigs are a great deal smarter than dogs but not as attractive to the human eye; it is assumed that it was for the sake of appearances that the gundog pig went out of fashion. Imagine turning up at a shoot beautifully turned – out in well tailored, bottle-green togs with a big, fat sow trotting to heel. Sure to glean a few unkind remarks, 'Looks damn bad don't it, damn bad'.

It does go to show just how well we got to know some of our fellow animals. The old countryman knew his animals well and there must have been a pretty strong bond between man and

pig that they should sally forth to go shooting together. Nowadays hardly anyone gets to know a pig really well. They have largely ceased to be friends and we have no contact with them. Instead, we put them into ghastly concentration camps and stuff them with food until they are worth their weight in pork. They live only a few months and in that time we don't bother to get to know them.

The creatures that we still know a bit about are the milk cows. The milk cow, the most generous of animals, gives her all without complaint for nothing – well, just her keep. Many years ago I was a farm manager of a 2,000 acre farm in Wiltshire. We had six separate milking herds and the cows were milked by machine out in the open. Probably the most uncomfortable job on the farm was to be a milker in this open-air milking parlour. There you shared along with the milk cow, the uncomfortable weather conditions that they had to put up with every day of the year. There was no time to go larking about at five o'clock on a filthy, black, February morning, with the icicles hanging about like organ pipes and a screeching north-eastern wind that slashed and cracked you chilblains. Your patience was sorely tested in these conditions but one thing was for certain, it was character-forming. Now the cows had their own pecking order, those who wanted to be milked first had to be milked first and in turn qualify for their ration of concentrated food for which they had waited all night. Sometimes the pecking order would be challenged. A young heifer would jump the queue and there would be an 'argy-bargy'. The vacuum cups would get knocked off, the electric fence short circuited and the whole herd would be off, across the field. It was times like these that you really wanted to kill something and sometimes you had to count, very slowly, up to 10,000 in order to stay your hand from doing something dreadful. Then, once you had calmed down, you had to start all over again and search about for the herd in pitch darkness, and round them up. And by now it was snowing, only looking on the bright side would help, when it snows it often becomes a little bit warmer.

I felt that I had to describe the horrors of open milking parlours so that you could appreciate the pressures that are put upon the cowmen who milk and look after their individual herds. Some of these cowman got very excited, some were coldly brutal, and some just lost their tempers and went barmy, screaming and shouting, laying about them with sticks on anything that moved. It is not a bit surprising that the character of each individual cowman was imprinted on his herd. If ever I came across a stray cow that had found a hole in the fence and wandered away I knew pretty well which herd she belonged to. If she spotted you and started searching for an escape route then that was one of Charlie's cows – excitable and unsure. If she took one look at you, turned and belted-off down the lane, blundering through nettles and brambles then that was surely one of Jim's cows going barmy just like he would do. But if you found one that was just browsing down a hedgerow and went on browsing until you got up to her, patted her rump, and would not move until you actually shoved her and made a few sharp noises then that was surely one of George's cows. George was as calm as a mill pond. The cow that saw you coming a long way away and as you got nearer, moved off slowly, keeping a good ten yards between us both all the time then it could be that she had suffered a bit of cold brutality at some stage. Could not say for sure but it may be one of Fred's cows.

Cows are sensitive and impressionable creatures, and it's quite clear that the attitude and behaviour of humans who look after them, are transmitted to the cows. An excitable and unstable man will, in time, create a cow with a similar character. And in a milking herd of 60 cows he will surely mould 30 tons of excitable and unstable cows.

The scientists and the slippery slide-rule-slickers were always telling us that a balanced ration of concentrates would produce a certain number of gallons of milk per day. They assured us that they were right because you could measure food and in turn measure the milk that was produced: anything that you can measure is bound to be right. But there are more important things that you cannot measure with accuracy such as the calm

100

cows of George's herd always produced far more milk than the other herds and they were feed on the same ration. The term 'Contented Cows' was coined years ago. Of course, I am talking about conditions of 40 years ago long before the efficient and clinical milking parlours had spread their automatic and steely, calm throughout the land. No doubt much of the temperamental human element will now have disappeared. It could be that the cow, like the clever pig of old, will disappear totally into a world of automation and anonymity. We are changing for better, or for worse, and the animals are changing with us. The more inert we become, the more zombie-like the animals we control become. Of one thing there is little doubt, we are in control and in charge, as we progress we seem to generally mess things up and I can only assume that the prospect for animals and for us is not all that rosy.

I have mentioned before that I am an anthropomorph – I view animals as people – and being an anthropomorph, you do bring certain stresses upon yourself. Of all the dreadful things that I have done – we all do dreadful things before experience and maturity pull us together – the most dreadful of all was what I did on a Monday morning. Monday was market day, and on these days I used to take the calves to market.

Now just to remind you of the fundamentals of milk production. A cow has a calf, and produces milk for that calf. We want the milk and so we take the calf away and sell it and in turn we milk the cow. To say the least, it is a disgusting and dirty trick and because of my feelings, I dreaded every Monday morning. I used to take a trailer and go to each milking herd to take away the calves that had been born during the week. And at every herd we acted out a dreadful Greek drama. The chorus would start a low moaning and wailing and the mothers whose children were being dragged away to be slaughtered sobbed and called, 'My child, my child please save my child'. I felt that I was the blinking villain of the piece. The mothers would run after the trailer as I drove away absolutely demented. 'Our children are going to die, so our lifes are also at an end, we too want to die, take us, kill us as well for life is not worth living without the precious children we have borne. Oh ye Gods, ye Gods, what have we done to deserve this'. It really was a Greek drama and I played the perpetual villain. It was perhaps significant that George's cows, were the most distressed of all. As George used to say: 'They do so terribly take on'.

The excitable herd and the barmy herd didn't seem to take on quite so much. I suppose they were so confused and muddled that they didn't know what was going on but George's cows just couldn't believe that we human beings, whom they had trusted and obeyed, could behave in such a despicable manner. They were heart-broken. I can never forget those Monday mornings and those distraught cows, they really did seem to take on much of the human character, a mother in distress.

The most bewildering and amazing association I have ever witnessed between man and animals was between a Senor Sangrino and the beasts he kept in his large garden. I am still not quite sure how I came to visit Senor Sangrino, it may have been because it was known that I was interested in animals and the natives in that part of the world knew quite a lot about Senor Sangrino's animals and thought I would be interested. Indeed, they were of great interest. Senor Sangrino lived in Patagonia and his large garden merged with the slopes of the Andes. It was a wild part of the world and the place's nature was tempered by the tremendous slopes of the Andes and the Condors that floated around. These great black undertakers who are always on the look out for corpses. You are always compelled to keep an eye on the sky in Patagonia for the Condors are often there and always follow in the path of death. Therefore, I didn't like the way that the two Condors that were circling high above Senor Sangrino's mountain garden as something close at hand had cleary succumbed. Senor Sangrino came stumbling, staggering out to meet me.

First impressions are sometimes very wrong but my first impression of Senor Sangrino was that he was as nutty as a fruit cake and in many ways a dangerous man, for it was clear that

103

he was not fully in control, neither of his body nor of his brain. He walked at a terrific speed, indeed so fast his legs could scarcely keep up with him. Certainly, I couldn't keep up with him and so he had to keep turning around to talk to me. The strange thing was that he would not simply turn his head back in my direction but he would complete the whole round turn with his entire body, so, that he sort of staggered and spun like a top that was running down and about to start lolling in a fit on the floor. He was being carried along by some barmy centrifugal force.

And as he tottered and spun and I jogged along behind we were harrassed by six enormous hounds that leapt and bounded all over us; they also looked half mad. These hounds had been specially bred to hunt wild boar and like most hunting dogs that I have met, you know in your heart-of-hearts that you have no true contact with them. You can see in their eyes, that distant, impersonal look that tells you that they are not completely in control and should a two-year old toddle across their line of vision they would eat it for breakfast. No wonder the Condors stuck around up there – sure to be good pickings hereabouts. And so I really became worried when we rounded a corner and walked straight into a mountain lion. The mountain lion (puma or cougar as it is known) is quite a formidable animal quite capable of knocking off a flock of sheep in a matter of minutes. Like the fox, it becomes so stimulated by the panic of the wretched animals baying in anguish as they cannot escape from their pens, that it just goes on killing and killing, obeying an instinct that would only rarely be aroused in open country where there were no convenient penned up flocks of animals. A fox is addicted to chickens as the mountain lion is to sheep although the latter a good deal larger and heavier. A mountain lion is quite a big cat to blunder into and it puckers its nose and releases its safety valve with a horrible hiss. It is meant to frighten and by jingo it does!

Senor Sangrino stopped spinning for a moment, saying 'It's only playing it likes to play with the hounds'. Its the most

dangerous sort of play that I have seen. The hounds leaping and slobbering around the mountain lion while it hissed and smacked away at anything and anyone who got anywhere near it. Very soon somebody was going to lose their temper and someone was going to get hurt. The Condors intelligent birds, had already lowered their altitude a couple of hundred feet. Then once more, Senor Sangrino started spinning; the hounds left the mountain lion to follow him down a path and into a small paddock. There standing was the ugliest and biggest wild boar I have ever seen – except that he didn't stand for long. He came belting across the field trying to get his strike in first, if he can.

Now wild boars are not funny. They were never meant to be. They carry a couple of flick knives with them in the form of tusks and they slash away to the left and right shredding a leg to ribbons just by casually nodding their heads. I don't mind admitting that I was much frightened until the dreadful hounds raced towards the boar. In a couple of bounds they were on the boar, grabbed it from behind by its hocks and holding it firm, so that it couldn't move. The hounds made no attempt to kill the boar, indeed they would have a job on as normally they just hold it and the boar is killed by the huntsman. But this boar is never killed. The hounds are called off and the boar trots back up to the paddock. He is the hounds sparring partner, the practice on him and judging by some of the old gashes on the hounds, he has put in a bit of practice on them himself. Perhaps I was wrong about Senor Sangrino, could it be that he was more in control than I had imagined. He certainly had some control over his dreadful hounds who in turn controlled the wild boar however there wasn't a great deal of control over the mountain lion who freely roamed around the garden playing with the hounds. I don't think the mountain lion liked it at all.

I would not care to wander alone in Senor Sangrino's garden especially with a couple of Condors up aloft on watch. But then I'm careful. I don't take risks certainly not silly risks like playing around with mountain lions. On the other hand I'm not as careful as the man whom I saw in Veracruz in Mexico.

106

He took a long time to decide but in the end he bought himself a pet from a man who was selling them in a street market. He was selling beetles as pets. Beetles as big as the top joint of your thumb and covered in jewels. Not real jewels of course, imitation emeralds, rubies and diamonds stuck with glue to the beetles back. From it's horny black left-hind leg trailed a fine gold chain and a tiny clip so that you can anchor him down wherever you please. He told me that these beetles were very nice to keep. You could keep them on a table or wear them on a dress so that you had a most wonderful mobile jewel that glistened in the sun and was admired by everybody.

That particular sort of beetle only ate wood and with each beetle, a whole year's supply of wood was given. Think of it, a pet that only ate wood. He asked me if I wanted one but I declined, saying that I didn't want one as I didn't like to see animals chained up in such a way.

Then he shattered me with a short lecture on the attributes of keeping a beetle on a chain compared to the disadvantages of keeping a poodle on a chain. Ladies have poodles with jewelled collars. Poodles can cost up to 1,000 dollars and eat all the time, they like to run about and bark. Beetles don't do that. They are quiet and they don't run about and only costs 75 cents. He was presenting a perfectly logical case. Only a fool would buy a poodle with a jewelled collar costing 1,000 dollars when you could buy a beetle for next to nothing. Only a fool would buy a poodle that needed exercise, yapped and ate filet steak, when you could buy a silent beetle that ate a scrap of wood.

'You buy a bootiful beetle Senor?'

He was watching me carefully, knowing that his argument was having some effect. His black, smooth hair was shining in the sun. His thick, eyebrows were bushy, and shaded his eyes, when he lifted his hand to smooth his black moustache, I saw that his hand was glittering with jewelled rings.

'You buy a bootiful beetle Senor'.

'No thanks'.

He was not a bit put out; his dark bland, face said absolutely nothing. The jewelled fingers carefully unwrapped a stick of chewing gum and passed it into his mouth and he began to slowly chew as he watched me. He was a human beetle.